# HERBS AND ALCHEMY

## TECHNIQUES FROM ANCIENT HERBAL LORE

### C. L. ZALEWSKI

PRISM · UNITY

*Dedications*
*for*
*"PERSIS"*

Published in Great Britain in 1990 by
PRISM PRESS
2 South Street,
Bridport,
Dorset, DT6 3NQ

and distributed in the USA by
ATRIUM PUBLISHERS GROUP
3356 Coffey Lane,
Santa Rosa, CA 95403

and published in Australia 1990 by
UNITY PRESS,
P.O. Box 532,
Woollahra,
NSW 2025

1 85327 046 6

Copyright © 1990, C. L. Zalewski

All rights reserved. No part of this publication may be reproduced, stored in
a retrieval system, or transmitted, in any form or by any means, electronic,
mechanical, photocopying, recording or otherwise, without the prior
permission of the publishers.

Printed and bound in the Channel Islands
by The Guernsey Press Company Limited.

# TABLE OF CONTENTS

# ACKNOWLEDGEMENTS

My thanks to my husband Pat Zalewski for his constant encouragement and help in all of my writings, and to the following individuals who each in some way influenced the outcome of this small book: Alison Lattey, Jack Taylor, Percy Wilkinson, and of course Mum.

# PREFACE

When this work was first conceived in 1980 by my wife Chris it was at a time when there was sparse literature available on the subject, and even today, with the exception of Scott Cunningham's excellent work, books such as this are few and far between. As a professional herbalist with a growing practice, as well as an excellent astrologer and an even better occultist, Chris is very well suited to the task of writing a book such as this. Her knowledge on Herbal Alchemy is not theoretical like some authors, but is in fact based on practical laboratory work, the results of some of which have been utilised as medicines for her Herbal practice. The Astral contact with the plants through clairvoyance also goes into a relatively new area that is original in its concept, and is not based on previous experiences of others but on a personal observation. Not only is she a Golden Dawn Adept but she is equally well versed and interested in Wiccan Craft, and it is in part to the latter that this book was structured and not merely for those working in Hermetic Orders. There will be some differences in the herbal associations here when compared to other works, and on this the reader will have to make up his or her mind which system to use. Since herbal and astrological associations are numerous it must be remembered that a herb applied magically and one for medicinal purposes may not always be the same.

Since this is not primarily a book on Alchemy, this has been covered only briefly with some additional information in certain areas which have not been published before. In recent years there has been a lot of publicity about alchemy and the Golden Dawn and what exactly they did teach, though nothing has been fully revealed on the subject. Originally the Golden Dawn was concerned mainly with Ritual Alchemy

5

and did not teach Practical Alchemy; it concerned itself with the impregnation of vital forces and left the students to make their own way with the practical method. Today, however, this has changed greatly as Practical Alchemy is taught along with the Ritual. Most of the practical usage comes from the works and students of Frater Albertus and his Paracelsus Organisation (which is now defunct in the USA though continues in Australia). The difference is that the Golden Dawn do not use the Kabbalistic system of Frater Albertus but that of the Order; also their astrological and ritual work are completely different and do not match the Frater Albertus system.

This book in its original format is also mandatory reading for Golden Dawn students as part of their 5=6 training, both in New Zealand and in some temples of the American branch of the Order. Overall the book is an excellent introduction to both the magical use of herbs and the ritual aspect of alchemy, and is something that could be built on by every person who studies, to suit their own individual temperament.

Pat Zalewski

# INTRODUCTION

I have held with considerable respect a very old teaching called 'Herbal Lore' used in the kitchen, in medicine and in magic. Many discard its importance, and many recognise its importance but do not make the effort to utilize it correctly.

My first introduction to herbal magic in any systemised form was through an Order called the Smaragdum Thallases, which is better known from its earlier name, the Golden Dawn. I received papers on astrological, Kabbalistical, and herbal associations which later I discovered were part of a manuscript called the *Book of Correspondences* that had been compiled by Mathers and other members of the Order. This manuscript, by the way, after the break up of the Order in England in the 1900s, had been published by Aleister Crowley under the title of *777* with some additions of his own.

Although I had always held an interest in Wiccan Craft, the Order radically changed my views on herbal use, synthesising the knowledge of Nature Craft with Hermeticism until now, for me, the two are inseparable. I originally wrote this book as a reference manual for personal workings, as I found no current literature in this part of the world at the time to provide such information in a condensed form. Since then the manual has remained part of my library, until such time as I was encouraged by my husband and Israel Regardie to publish. Just recently, while preparing this introduction, Scott Cunningham's works on magical herbalism were brought to my attention. I found his work very informative, but decided to go ahead with publication as my work appeared not to repeat Cunningham's work but to add to it, and in some areas, such as alchemy, go more in depth but from a different perspective—a Hermetic approach. What I did not do, though, was improve my cataloguing of herbs from my original draft, as I saw no need to repeat what had already been published in Cunningham's encyclopedia.

In the following text I have endeavoured to lay out guidelines and instructions on how one goes about using herbs in magic and alchemy. Spagyric medicine includes the use of herbs, but I have not included spagyric herbal medicine in this text as the subject is so vast that, to do it justice, more than one volume would need to be written, and there are current publications on herbs and homoeopathy which already cover the subject adequately.

One may ask 'what is magic in alchemy?' and 'how do herbs apply?' I hope to unfold the answers to these questions gradually in the following chapters, but first I would like to point out that magic is life, creation and the creative; magic is in the air; magic is everywhere—everything we think or do is magic. Magic in alchemy is the concentration of life's energies through the Will, manipulating and working in harmony the vibrations of creation of our planet with the cosmic forces that be, into a desired object. The operation is ritual, whether it be on a large scale with full ceremony or just acted out in the mind.

I have endeavoured to collate the 'scattered' available material on herbs and their planetary, zodiac and element correspondences, and to provide a brief listing and definition of the methods by which herbs were used in magic, together with some recipes of such. The chapters on harvesting, alchemy and ritual workings provide guides on how one goes about making their products magical. As for the magical harvesting/picking times of herbs, general agricultural cultivation information is suitably explained in other available publications. What I have supplied are guidelines to aid in the preparations of the *magical* harvesting. Each herb has its own 'special time' and vibration, therefore to aid the practitioner in locating that 'special time' a chapter is included which should, along with the correspondences from Chapter 5, prove sufficient.

With the technical information given in the following chapters, and applied intellectually with a general understanding of astrology, use of intuition, common sense and vibrations, one should be reasonably successful in choosing the herb(s) for a defined purpose. But the success of a product and purpose of the use of herb depends entirely on the individual and the manner of application. This will be explained later.

In relating a herb to a godform, compare the deity with the planetary, zodiac and element nature. 'Like' natures attract 'like' vibrations. This method has proven quite satisfactory in past workings. Do not pair opposites in any event, whether it be the mixing of herbs or oils, the herb to the purpose of use, or, for example, an aggressive godform with a passive herb. Your experiment will not work, or will turn out disastrously.

An understanding of the planets, signs and elements and their harmonies and frictions is very important to ensure your success. With careful use and study of herbs one can utilise such knowledge in all activities. This knowledge can open many doors, unleashing a power, but at the same time one must be able to control this power. The growing, picking and working of herbs to the law of nature is a task that needs great patience—time is on nature's side. Operating at harmonious astrological times includes not only the actual making of the product, but extends from the inception of an idea to final use.

It has been said that if you wait for the right astrological time to do your working you would be waiting for ever, and that any time should be satisfactory, for it is the operator's Will that is of importance. On the one hand I agree wholeheartedly with this, and on the other hand I do not. It all depends again on *what* you are doing and, most importantly, what your psyche needs. One could go on for quite some time on the pros and cons of specifics, so I leave the decision up to the reader, relying on their inner sight to see what working should or should not be done in a particular way. Experience will teach you, and you get experience only by experimenting. I will emphasise, though, that the reader should take heed of the advice given in the chapter on harvesting. There *is* a right and wrong time to pick particular plants.

The alchemy section is a brief summary of some methods of herbal alchemy. The Z2 ritual has been included to give an idea of the application of ritual magic in alchemy. This method can be designed as a quick or slow method. Some may take up to three years on an experiment while others up to six months or less—maybe only seven days. It all depends on the practitioner and the desired effect. A great deal has *not* been added for specific reasons, but what has been provided should be a satisfactory springboard for the reader. Simplicity is the key.

Hopefully I have provided clear guidelines in which you can work. I say 'guidelines', for guidelines and correspondences should be sufficient to aid an individual in tuning in to what and how they must operate.

One of the curiosities of recent years has been the degree of alchemy as practised within the Golden Dawn. Recently Ellic Howe published *The Ayton Papers*, which were rumoured to reveal all about Golden Dawn alchemical procedure. Though well researched by Howe the material was in fact a bitter disappointment, and did not even scratch the surface of alchemical procedures. Mrs Felkin, who at one time was an unofficial head of the Stella Matutina, had commented to one of the Order members in New Zealand that studies of this type were eventually abandoned. Alchemy was divided into two camps within the Golden Dawn—metallic and herbal. This book talks about the herbal side of alchemy, and has a relationship to medicinal use which was used by Dr Berridge, and an astral connection with plants and herbs as experimented on by Florence Farr. Dr Berridge, a homoeopathist of course, used many alchemical experiments in connection with the theories of Hanemann, which were closely allied with alchemy. Florence Farr, on the other hand, experimented in plant contact which she considered was more important (in some instances) than the experiment itself. She also experimented in herbal tinctures and wrote some minor papers on it. I have attempted to bring out in this present book the concepts of Florence Farr in plant contact, and Dr Berridge (who also, like Steiner, experimented in Etheric tinctures) in his work.

# CHAPTER ONE
# MAGICAL USE

The term Magical Use suggests the following:
Incense, Oil, Balsam (Salve), Dry Burning, Wet Burning, Sacrificial, Talismatic, Emblems, Sachet Mixtures, Sleep Pillows, Dry Use, Alchemy (note: alchemy is not just the working of metals), Garden Magic, Aromatics, Perfume, Flowers, Fire Worship, Psychic Correspondence, Woodbase, Wood, Potion (Philtre), Bath, Dyes, Candles, Divination.

A definition of the above is given in the following text. Although there are many ways in which a herb can be used magically that are not listed above, most of them would come under the given headings.

### Incense

Aromatic gum or resin, wood, bark, oil or other substance producing a sweet odour when burned. Incense is commonly known as a dried powdered herb or wood of a herb, which is formed into hard cones, sticks or tiny pebbles. There is a great variety of recipes and methods by which incense can be made. An incensed atmosphere is considered a suitable environment for an evoked spirit or force to manifest itself; for an effect on the psyche; for attraction of planetary and zodiac force. It is, in fact, an essential part of the success of ritual, and it is important that the right incense is used: for example, a fish does not swim in air, it must have water, thus a water-related force must have a water-related incense.

### Oil

Oil is an extract from a plant or part of a plant. A substance typically unctuous, viscous, combustible, liquid at ordinary temperatures, and soluble in ether or alcohol but not in water. It is used for lubricating, illuminating (flames giving off scent), anointing, perfumes, etc. Anointing oils are a major part of rituals and, in fact, the anointing is a ritual in itself.

### Balsam

Fragrant drippings from certain trees and plants; balm; an oleoresin; an aromatic ointment; a 'rub' which covers the operator's body or object of purpose. Magical ointments were made from narcotics and/or hallucinogenic herbs which gave the feeling of flying, etc. These ointments were rubbed over the body and under the armpits, because the drug was absorbed through the skin, especially in areas of soft skin. In that way the practitioner would be less likely to suffer from acute poisoning and stomach upsets by taking herbs as a potion.

### Dry Burning

Dried leaves, wood, flowers or all of a herb are burnt in a fire. The smoke from such a fire has an aromatic scent, used as offerings, purifying of air, warding off danger, etc.

### Wet Burning

As Dry Burning, but the herb has been freshly cut and the wood, flowers and foliage are still green.

### Sacrificial

Wet, dry, as incense, powdered or liquid. Burning of herbs as in offerings; casting to the wind; running away in water; all are forms of gestures which could be sacrificial. The 'intent' of the operator is the key.

### Talismatic

Talismans are fumed for consecration by incense; oiled by perfumed oil, etc. The talisman is exposed to the herb in the correct hours of the correct day of the planet to whom the talisman is dedicated.

### Emblems

Emblems are objects of representation; good luck charms; badges. Make and form of emblems are numerous. Majority of the time a herb is worn as a form of protection.

### Sachet Mixtures

Emblems. These sachets contain dried herbs, which are of a scent. Common use, apart from domestic, is to hang in suitable places to keep undesirables away.

### Sleep Pillows

Pillows filled with a certain herb or herbs which encourage a particular phenomenon during sleep, when sleeping on them or with them under one's main pillow.

### Dry Use

Sprays of herb or herbs used as representative of a force or meaning. For example, see Rose, or Acacia.

### Alchemy

Many forms of alchemic experiments can be formed with herbs: cooking is a simple form; combining them; using them to draw forces etc.; making oils; balsam; incense. The major use of herbs in alchemy is the use of herbs in healing—mixing of medicine (tinctures) and healing salves, etc. The cure is obtained by using the opposing forces, negative against positive, an ailment being the negative and the curative agents being the positive. Manifestation occurs when the two forces meet. Basically, the object of herbal alchemical remedies is to supplement forces lacking in the human body, thereby giving a balance.

### Garden Magic
Plants grown in strategical positions in the garden perform certain tasks. For example, see Rosemary and Sage. Many herbs respond to impending weather changes.

### Aromatics
Plant or drugs which yield a fragrant smell. Incense; oil; balsam; perfume, etc.

### Perfume
A substance which emits a pleasing odour. Used in ritual on person or object of operation. Normally made from the flowers of a herb. Emits power over senses; fulfils almost every canon of the magical arts. It has power over moods and strong psychological effects; power to influence the imagination. Perfume comes in all forms, liquid, dried, solid, semi liquid, etc. Perfumery should be rated high in magical arts for it exerts a command over the whole range of human emotions. The magician who learns its secrets acquires power to unlock the door of his own personality, becoming thereby the master of Yin and Yang.

### Flowers
Used as symbology and perfume. A wreath is used as a magic circle to protect or bind the deceased spirit and soul, preventing it from haunting the living.

### Fire Worship
Incense and fire worship incantation:

> 'Fire, fire, blessed fire,
> Unto my will I aspire,
> So I hope that I may see,
> My desire come to me.'

Superstitious peasants used to light large fires on hill tops to protect their communities from psychic attack. These forces served as a fumigation against witches or devils, etc. The ashes of the fires were thought to contain supernatural powers and were used by psychic healers.

### Psychic Correspondence

This refers to the correspondence of astrological and other forces to a herb, and emphasises a psychic affect.

### Woodbase

Incense made from sawdust of wood.

### Wood

Used in the making of implements or equipment for magical purposes.

### Potion

Infusion taken as a tea.

### Bath

Herbal baths are taken before ritual. This is a form of purification.

### Dyes

Dyes prepared magically are used in colouring implements and drawing sigils, seals, for ritual clothes, etc.

### Candles

Prepared herbs or extracts of herbs can be used in candle making, or after the candle has been made by anointing the candle with a herbal anointing oil made specifically for the purpose.

# CHAPTER TWO
# CLASSIFYING HERBS

Herbs are categorised into botanical families. These are: Rosaceae, Liliaceae, Umbelliferae, Labiatae, Papilionaceae, Cruciferae, Compositae. The three major groups are the Mints (Labiatae), the Carrot/Parsley group (Umbelliferae), and the Daisy group (Compositae).

In the **Labiatae** family there are herbs such as Balm, Basil, Catnip, Hyssop, Lavender, Marjoram, Mints, Oregano, Pennyroyal, Rosemary, Sage, Thyme, etc., and these have typical square stems, simple leaves and, among the leaves, two-lipped flowers that grow in whorls.

In the **Umbelliferae** family there are herbs such as Angelica, Anise, Caraway, Dill, Fennel, Parsley, etc., which have stems that are cylindrical and usually hollow. Flowers form in flat-topped umbells.

In the **Compositae** family are herbs such as Lads Love, Marigold, Mugwort, Tansy, Tarragon, Wormwood, etc., and these herbs have flowers which are ray or disk shaped, for example daisies, dandelions.

Other families are the Boraginaceae family, the Lauraceae family, the Rutaceae and the Violaceae families.

Other forms of classification are:

### Solar Cycle
Annuals are like the Sun which passes through the zodiac in one year. These herbs would show a character towards the sun, being large, golden or orange, orbicular shaped, radiating, with an aromatic odour, an action on the heart and a tendency to turn towards the sun; for example, the Sunflower, the red orange spice Saffron and the Marigold.

17

### Lunar Cycle

Herbs with soft juicy leaves, often live in fresh water. The flowers and fruit are white or pale yellow and the fruits are large, watery and tasteless; for example, the Pumpkin and Gourd. These herbs show monthly periodicity and moon shapes.

### Mercury Cycle

Mercury has a 3-month cycle through the zodiac. Its herbs have fine or highly divided leaves or stems, an airy nature like grasses, and a subtle odour; for example, Anise. They are also high in mineral and vitamin content, like Parsley.

### Venus Cycle

Venus moves through the zodiac in nine months, and its herbs have beautiful flowers, white or pink, a pleasant odour and smooth green foliage. They may have fruits.

### Mars Cycle

Mars passes through the zodiac every two years and this sign was formerly used for biennials. The plants possess thorns, spines or prickles, grow in dry harsh areas and have acrid, pungent or stimulating odours; for example, Raspberry or Red Pepper. They have a cornical root (tap root); for example, Carrot, Beet.

### Jupiter Cycle

It takes Jupiter twelve years to pass through the zodiac, and this is how long these perennials live. These herbs are herbaceous perennials and show the signature of the cross, they are large and conspicuous, edible and nutritious; for example, Fig, Olive, Grape, Acorn, Beech-nut. Their odour is pleasant.

### Saturn Cycle

Saturn completes its course in thirty years. Woody Perennials often live thirty years, some live longer. These plants show annual rings, grey or dull foliage or bark, and are usually woody. They have an unpleasant taste and odour, are often poisonous and have a cooling affect.

### Uranus Cycle

Hybrid plants, cornfields, plants that can be transplanted.

### Neptune Cycle

Seaweed, plants *under* water, Opium, Water mosses, Fungi, Hallucinogenic plants.

### Pluto Cycle

Evergreen trees, weeds, drug-yielding plants, poisonous plants and rejuvenating plants. Mosses, Marshes, Cedar Trees, Palm Trees.

Classification can also be under tender annuals, hardy annuals, biennials, tender perennials and hardy perennials.

Another form of planetary association is to compare the herbs which medically affect or treat the human bodyparts to the planet and sign which rule those parts. First the planets:

### Sun

Heart, spine (upper portion), right eye of male, left eye of female, vitality, fevers, bilious affections, eye disorders, swooning, circulation, upper portion of back.

### Moon

Stomach, breast, left eye of male, right eye of female, feminine complaints, fluidic derangements, stomach affections, digestion, dropsy, tumours, abscesses, cold, epilepsy.

## Mercury

Anxiety, lungs, shoulders, arms, hands, diet, nervous disorders, mental, speech, headaches, solar plexus.

## Venus

Neck, chin, vocal chords, neck and throat, hymen, haemorrhoids, bladder, hair, cysts, swellings, diphtheria, renal disorders, syphilis, laxity of muscle tissue, interior generative system.

## Mars

Fever, inflammation, headaches, skull, face, arteries, external sex organs, operations, wounds, burns, nasal, muscular and genital disorders, contagious diseases in general, gall, left ear.

## Jupiter

Liver, thighs, diabetes, disorders of blood, dental problems, pleurisy, boils, abscesses.

## Saturn

Knees, skin, bones, spleen, teeth, hearing, rheumatism, gout, bronchitis, paralysis, deafness, hypochondria, consumption, gangrene, flu, spinal maladies.

## Uranus

Ankles, X-rays, spasmodic disorders, ruptures, strictures, cramp, shock, hiccough, ruling action of parathyroid, gases, pupils of eyes, nervous system (electrical energies).

## Neptune

Blood, body fluids, feet, coma, lethargy, poisoning, hallucination, trance, ruling part of parathyroid, pineal, toxins, spinal canal.

**Pluto**
Suicide, sex quotient, depression, rules the third eye, stellar healing.

Now the signs:

**Aries**
Head, face.

**Taurus**
Neck, throat and larynx.

**Gemini**
Arms and lungs, shoulders, nervous system.

**Cancer**
Stomach and chest.

**Leo**
Spine, back and heart.

**Virgo**
Bowels and fingers.

**Libra**
Kidneys, loins, lumbar and skin.

**Scorpio**
Generative system, genitals, urinary organs and lower
   bowels.

**Sagittarius**
Hips, thighs, buttocks.

**Capricorn**
Knees, bones.

**Aquarius**
Legs and ankles.

**Pisces**
Feet, fluids, lymphatics.

# CHAPTER THREE
# HARVESTING FOR MAGIC

'a time for everything'

'For everything there is a season and a time for every purpose; a time to plant and a time to harvest. Convenient times are chosen to plant according to the increase and decrease of the moon and with aspects of the moon unto such planets as most aptly serve a particular plant.' This must also be with harvesting.

The time to harvest depends entirely on what is required of a herb and the individual plant's cycle. Spring is the time when the entire plant is in its most full perfection, when in the bud, and when the heads are formed for flowering but not yet fully opened. This is the time when the volatile oil content is highest. For the Southern Hemisphere it begins in Virgo, goes through Libra and into Scorpio, and for the Northern Hemisphere Pisces, Aries and Taurus. In general this is the season of most dominance in harvesting for magical use. The time of day most appropriate for harvest is dawn, when a plant is at its height of vitality—a high content of sap and vital fluid. But, again, this depends on the herb and its analogies.

The law of analogy should always be observed, therefore the season, day, purpose for which the herb is required, and the astrological associations to the herb, combined with the current planetary movements, must all be taken into consideration before harvesting. Along with these points the day must be fine and clear, and the harvester purified in mind and body. Meditational exercises and a purification bath would suffice.

A guideline is set out below to which one can work when harvesting herbs for magic. The care spent on the picking of a plant is vitally important. As has been proven by Kirlian photography, a healthy plant has intense, dynamic, vital energy in and surrounding it. In fact, a plant has an aura just as animal life, and this vital force must be captured to make any alchemical experiment worthwhile.

1    Locate plant or plants to be used. Clear away surrounding weeds and draw a magical circle around the area, vibrating the names of the 'art', purifying the area of any element which could harm the operation. Converse with the herb, telling it what is to happen and what is expected of it, ordering it to draw greater force from the ground to aid in the operation.

2    Frequent the site(s) to observe progress.

3    At time of harvest, draw another circle around the previous circle through the method of the 'art', then harvest according to the 'rules'.

### Basic Rules and Handy Hints

For 'wet use' (fresh plant), harvest at dawn while dew is still on the plant, just before the sun comes up.

For drying purposes, harvest at dawn when the dew has *just* evaporated, before the day sets in.

The exceptions to harvesting at dawn are listed with the individual herbs in Chapter 5.

The season to harvest depends entirely on the requirements. For example, ripened fruit and seeds would be collected in Capricorn, Aquarius and Pisces for the Southern Hemisphere, and Cancer, Leo and Virgo for the Northern Hemisphere.

Harvest in the planetary hour and day analogous to the herb.

Synchronise the time of harvest with harmonious planetary movements.

An Electional or Horary horoscope can be drawn up to obtain more accuracy as to the astrological associations, the time and harmony of the commencement of the operation (see Astrological Guides, p. 30). One is able to see from the horoscope the progress of the operation, along with the opportune time to commence and complete each step throughout the duration of the task.

In harvesting the *whole* plant, one *does not* touch the plant with the bare hands, or any bodypart. The plant is tied to a larger plant (which springs back, pulling the herb out by the roots), or use a consecrated object. The earth is loosened around the roots before pulling. Immediately after the roots leave the soil an offering (grain and honey) is left in the broken earth to appease and deter the elementals from vamperising the vital force of the pulled plant.

No harvested plant should be placed back on the ground. The vital energies which must be trapped for magical use only, return to the ground if contact is made. This is the reason for not touching the herb with your bare skin, for the human body acts as a conductor earthing the vital forces.

In picking the leaves or tops of herbs, or in gathering the seed or sap, one *can* touch the herb with bare hands for the mother plant is still strong in her vital force, with her roots undisturbed and still in contact with the ground. It would be more beneficial, though, if you had specially prepared tools that will be gentle with the herb.

In drying herbs a high volatile oil content is important. The tops of the plant are always preferable to the whole plant for immediate use, and the time of the day for picking must be when the morning dew is dried away. If they be cut wet with dew, herbs will not dry well, and if they be cut at noon-day, when the sun has made the leaves flag, they will not have their full power.

The picking of a herb in the early morning after the dew has dried applies only when 'picking'. This, of course, does not apply when gathering the 'dew' and 'sap' from plants. I will stress the point that the 'dawn' and 'early morning' is considered a very powerful time for a plant (as is the spring season). This is a time when the sap has risen to its heights, the life source, the dew appears and the sap is excreted. Spring in itself is a time when the power of the life-force flows through the vegetation, which has a dynamic flush of growth.

'When the herbs are thus gathered they are to be looked over, the decayed leaves picked off, and the dead ends of the stalks cut away. They are then to be tied up in small bunches, the less the better, and hung upon lines drawn across the room where the windows and doors are to be kept open in good weather; the bunches ... are to hang till perfectly dry, They are then to be taken softly down without shaking off the buds of the flowers and laid evenly in a drawer, pressing them down and covering them with paper.' (Sir John Hill *The British Herbal* 1756)

Choose neither the large leaves nor the small leaves but the mean leaves, and pick the tops and sow when the moon is waxing, reap when the moon is waning. Sow root crops when the moon is waning.

Most important of all is that herbs, plants and flowers must be gathered with 'discretion' and respect, taking no more than necessary, carefully considering which part to pick. Talk silently to the plant, let it show you where to pick. It does this by creating a cold spot. Remember also to warn the plant of your intention so that it may prepare itself. This sort of meditation can prove beneficial. Tuning into the vibrations of plants can reveal a great many secrets as to the 'nature' of a plant.

Harvesting can be accomplished in many ways: by *gathering*— picking tops of the plants, collecting the seeds, gathering from the ground (e.g. nuts), etc; by *cutting*—where a plant is cut off at the base, the whole plant used after drying, or just the seeds dried and collected after the plant has been hung for a period of time; by *pulling*—like garlic, the plant and root pulled out when leaves are dead, in the fall. This is the time when the strength has gone down into the root. Dig them in early spring also before the sap rises; by *extracting*— making an incision to extract the gum (sap); and by *peeling*—bark from trunk, root or branch peeled from the young tree in autumn or early spring. The young bark is gently shaven off.

In the above examples the gathering, cutting and incision still ensures the survival of the main plant. When pulling, the plant is completely removed. The plant need not be destroyed, though, for a root cutting can be made and the new, small roots replanted. This is a good method for plants that are hard to grow from seed. Some cuttings can also be placed in water to develop their own roots, then planted. Bulbs or cloves, as in Garlic, are separated and replanted for the next season's crop.

Perennials should not be cut (picked) back as severely as the annuals, which are cut back to leave four inches of stem. Perennials must have no more than a third of their growth removed for drying or other use. The safest way is to take only the leafy tips. Harvest perennials carefully so as to promote growth (as in pruning).

Do not strip leaves off stems before drying, for they get bruised; keep the herbs separate and aired while picking, so that their volatile oil is not lost through heating. Flowers for drying must be fully open, although it is necessary that some varieties are collected while in bud. Another method of collecting seeds is when the flower heads are turned down—the heads are cut off into a paper bag and then taken to a drying area.

If the root of a herb is required, dig the root out when the leaves of the plant begin to die down, or when the biennial is two years old, or when the perennial is over two years old. Clean with a hose gun, do not scrape.

### Moon Cycle

The moon cycle described below may aid your harvesting times for magical purposes. While these phases may aid in your success, a plant's cycle may not coincide. For example, the seeds may not ripen or the flowers bloom. Careful planting and appropriate weather can bring about timely readiness of a plant, but in either case one can harvest only when the plant is ready and willing, then, during that phase if there is urgent need, a suitable moon-time may be decided. If the time is not fortuitous in all aspects for the success of your operation when the plant is ready, *do not* harvest; wait another cycle, or gather only the seeds for future planting and cycle planning for more harmonious conditions. (A greenhouse could be of great help here, but be very careful and observant if forcing growth.)

*New Moon Phase* This phase is considered a waxing phase, when everything feels an upsurge of energy. The moon rises and sets with the sun, and perhaps there is a duality of forces during this phase. The sap flow is upwards. It is warned that when picking plants at this phase one must take great care not to damage the main plant, for rotting takes place too easily; plants need more oxygen in this phase.

Plants are picked during the new moon phase according to their purpose of use. The nature of use in this instance would be: concerning the sun and moon equally; concerning the beginning of; to activate the first surge in a matter; to cause change. Annuals that produce above ground, especially the leafy kind that produce seeds outside the fruit, are the most responsive to this phase.

*First Quarter Moon Phase* The energy is rising; the sap flow is upwards. The moon rises now at noon and sets at midnight. It is a phase to activate the activities of the Balsamic Moon Phase. A good time to start anything. If the herbs were plucked during Balsamic Moon, now is the time to begin preparations for required use. Alchemic transformation of one stage to another is operated at this phase. The two days before full moon (last 2 days of 1st quarter) are considered good for picking if the nature of the operation demands.

The nature of this phase concerns: the reinforcing of a matter; adding strength to; to cause growth to; for success of a matter of the nature. The sun is strong, the moon is strengthening. Annuals above ground, especially the vine type with seeds inside, are very responsive.

**Full Moon Phase** This phase has a peaking of electro-magnetic energy in all living things at the exact time of full moon. The sap flow is downwards. For two days before full moon, and at full moon, are times when herbs are plucked for medicinal and culinary use. They are most potent medically. Some say now is the time for picking for magical use. One must also realise that this depends on the 'nature' of the herb, and operation for which the herb is picked.

The nature of this phase is: for attraction; to draw down; moon strongest. Perennials, biennials, bulb and root crops are especially responsive. The culmination of one's endeavours (full moon to the beginning of the last quarter).

**Last Quarter Moon Phase** This is a barren phase where it is most appropriate to rest and plan. The moon rises at midnight and vanishes in the morning, and only at that time can one undertake anything that requires a moon influence.

The nature of this phase is: to decrease; to culminate; terminate.

**Balsamic Moon Phase** The last three days before new moon, and the last three days of the last quarter moon phase.

A lot has been said about this stage being evil and a bad

time for anything, but some sources say that herbs for magical purpose should be picked now. This would fit in with the idea of the moon cycle being used for the preparation of a magical mixture and/or special activity (see moon cycle above).

The nature of this phase is that of the sun, so it would seem natural that those herbs of the sun be considered for picking now. However I do not entirely agree with this when one considers the full moon reflects the light of the Sun at night. It is known that if herbs be picked last quarter and Balsamic phase they hold their scent, so it would seem proper to pick during this phase if a product emitting a strong and lasting scent is required (such as incense), but this again must be carefully thought out according to the nature of the herb.

Another theory is that the Balsamic Moon phase is the culmination of all the powers collected by the completed moon cycle!

In either case the nature of this phase would be thus: the sun; to make a cycle complete; to attract or to stretch out to (i.e. the sap has reached bottom but not yet moved up, but moving up is inevitable and there is no other direction to go); a condition completely uninfluenced by the moon (under certain circumstances this could make a herb very versatile according to its planetary, zodiac and element nature).

### Astrological Guides
In casting an electional or horary horoscope:
— Fortify the nature of the herb(s) with the Lord of the Ascendant.
— For self development or medical (let the herb(s) be the same as the ascendant), fortify the herb(s) to the planet of your rising sign and make the nature of the herb(s) be in opposition to the planet ruling the 6th house. Strengthen the sick part of the body with herb(s) in harmony.
— Let the Lord of the 10th be strong.
— Let the Lord of the house most applicable to the nature

(purpose) of use be fortified along with such house.
— Fortify the moon, sun and ascendant, and significator must be further than 17° from the sun.
— Retrograde planets are considered malefics.
— In almost all cases avoid placing the sun and moon on the ascendant.
— Fortify Fortuna with dispositor.
— Pay special attention to the lunar aspects, and the sign and phase to which the moon is in.

The moon is weakened in ten ways:

1   Combust — within 12° from the sun, worst when applying than separating from aspect.
2   In Scorpio, especially 3° Scorpio, exact degree of fall.
3   12° each way when in opposition, especially when applying, not including aspect to the sun.
4   Conjunct, square or opposition to a malefic.
5   Within 12° of Caput or Cauda Draconis.
6   In later degrees of a sign which contains a malefic.
7   When cadent or via combusta.
8   In its detriment (Capricorn) or in Aries, or Libra.
9   Slow in motion—moving less than her average speed of 13° 11′ a day.
10  When void of course. (Performing no aspects when entering another sign.)

In all cases if possible place the moon in the house ruling the matter of election.

### Herbal Search

This exercise is a very necessary part of the magical use of herbs. Though known to some herbal alchemists, it was utilised by the Golden Dawn Society's Inner Order (when the Adept had proved his clairvoyant ability).

For example, if an Adept was about to work an alchemical ritual and had made the necessary astrological calculations, he or she would have to forge an astral link with the plant or plants about to be harvested. The reason for this was practical as well as alchemical. The first phase was the contact area, where the herbs are planted. The Adept would visit this area in the hope of establishing contact, by sitting quietly amongst the plants, mind reaching out to the type of herb that was required. The amount of times this was performed varied with the ability of the individual; from one sitting to five or more. Once a contact had been established the next step was to actually locate the exact herb in question. This is done by moving among the plants until the herb contacted is identified. Your mind links into the energy of the herb and acts as a type of radar homing device. When I speak of the 'mind' I am also referring to all the essential factors of one's being that aid in the detection of the herb. The mind in itself is just the central control.

The next step is to try and communicate with the plant itself, informing it of your intentions and giving it a chance to close off vital circuits in its stem and activate others. Here the herb willingly (if the empathy between you is harmonious) isolates some of its vital energy in certain parts of it, so that its main body is protected. When you pick the leaves in question, the cells are then closed and the vital energy does not escape. One small leaf harvested this way, in empathy with the plant, can equal in energy content up to twenty times its own weight compared to other leaves collected without this astral method of contact. About 30 minutes to an hour before the herb is picked the plant is informed that it is about to be picked, and to prepare itself. The ground is then cleared of negative

32

vibrations by the lesser banishing ritual of the pentagram of the Golden Dawn.

Some Adepti have been known to offer prayers to the elements to help. These invocations, relating to the elemental family to which the plant belongs, are included in the final part of the grade rituals of the Golden Dawn 1°=10° to 4°=7°.

To those who do not accept the spiritual value of communicating with nature many of these preparations are cumbersome and meaningless, but to the Adept they will be a great help. Clairvoyant analysis of this method of herb contact shows that the aura[1] of the Adept goes out and is accepted by the plant. This energy helps the plant accelerate the necessary opening and shutting procedure in its physiological system, so that the Adept can harvest it. In fact, the leaf used has part of the Adept's aura impregnated into it (through his aid to the plant), so that during the alchemic process the link is already there.

[1] The term "aura" is used loosely to represent one's "life-force".

# CHAPTER FOUR
# COMPANION HERBS

When planting herbs, certain types grow well together and certain types repel, just like people. Companion planting is a system evolved since the time of Pliny, which groups together the friendly plants to benefit one another. I include this subject on the theory that if plants disagree or agree in the ground, then they must also react in use (in mixtures of incense, sachets, etc.). This chapter is to aid you in preparing your formulae and to further the success of your operations.

Companion groupings can be explained quite logically by root levels in the soil which occur in nature; some roots also secrete a variety of organic substances which affect micro-organisms in surrounding ground; a great effect is made with the type of nutrients absorbed. There are mutually harmful plants when kept close to each other, such as Basil with Rue, Garlic with Beans and Peas, Sunflowers and Potatoes. Flowers, vegetables and herbs are planted together to give control over insect pests. They act as repellents to pests, while some attract the pests away from the vegetables, for example the Onion family (repellent). Certain herbs protect the garden from predators (for example, Chervil, Dill, Borage, Parsley, Sage, Tarragon and Thyme) by having repelling odours or foliage irritative to varieties of predators.

## Some Groupings and Repellents

Wormwood has toxic leaf and root excretions, thus no plants grow well near this herb; this also applies to Fennel.
Radish and Hyssop do not go well together.

34

Strawberries flourish under Borage leaves.
Figtree and Rue are great friends.
Savoury and Onion complement in growth.
Strawberry and Nettle thrive together.
Basil and Rue will not grow together.
Borage likes Tomatoes, Squash and Strawberries.
Anise mutually benefits Coriander and attracts cats and rats.
Balm is a great benefiter.
Caraway likes Peas and will cross-pollinate with Fennel.
Yarrow increases the aromatic qualities of medicinal and fragrant herbs.
Grow Hyssop with Grapes.
Dill goes with Cabbages but not with Carrots and Tomatoes.
Plant Fennel near your kennel and the powdered leaves or seeds keep away the fleas.
Garlic loves Roses, Raspberries and stonefruit, and vice versa.
Chives like Carrots, Roses and Apple trees, but not Peas and Beans.
Chamomile benefits all nearby herbs and plants.
Catnip deters flea beetle and mice but attracts cats.
Watch a Mint's roots.
Parsley aids Roses.
Pennyroyal repels ants and mosquitoes.
Rosemary and Sage, a great combination.
Tansy with Rose and Raspberry.
Lads Love grows with Rosemary and Lavender.
Tarragon is good throughout the garden.
Most of the above herbs act as insect repellants.

When combining herbs in mixes consider also their planetary and zodiac combinations. What complements what, what adversely affects what; this would include planetary rulership, fall, exaltation and detriment. Try to combine the herbs of 'like' nature, which in itself is essential for the nature of an operation.

# CHAPTER FIVE
# CORRESPONDENCES

The following is a listing of herbs, their attributions and magical use, plus other miscellaneous information, in brevity, referring to each herb.

There has been some concern as to the manner by which the astrological attributions were given. The manner I have standardised to is the application of planet and zodiac sign to the medicinal qualities of a herb, the visual appearance (you will see some reference to this on the herb cycles discussed earlier), and their capacity to bear fruit, flower and seed. Another method of attributing the zodiac is by growth cycles of each plant; in which month a plant flowers, etc. This is all well and good but very regional to climatic conditions, thereby requiring a listing of every place in latitude and longitude, soil conditions, etc., and as some plants do not grow in some countries unless under glasshouse conditions, this method can lead to great complication. This, of course, does not stop the home gardener from experimenting in the latter method.

The elements in brackets [e.g.($\triangle$ of $\triangle$)] are the 'nature' of the herb, and the elements not in brackets are the elements in which the 'elements of the nature' of the herb operate. The planets and signs in brackets are additional references which I found necessary to include due to the inability of various sources to agree on one planet or sign per herb. The planets and signs in brackets beside the Fixed Stars are those in accordance with such stars.

**Warning** When obtaining herbs for use externally or internally from the following listing, please refer to a good medical herb book to check the potency of the herbs, for some herbs may work as an irritant to a sensitive skin, and some are deadly poisonous. The recipes supplied in the following chapter have been tested and are proven, but for safety it is still recommended to check.

**Absinthe** *see* **Wormwood**

**Acacia** (Egyptian Thorn)
(△ of ▽) ▽ of ▽ ♂ ♏ (☿)          Woody Perennial
Balsam; wood; dry use; flower; perfume.
Re G.D. ceremonial and hermetic use, branch (spray) in
flower to symbolise the sacred word of the Hebrews. The
wood was used in building the Tabernacle.
Flowers—divination and trance work. Flowers used in love
magic.
Harvest mid-winter to mid-summer, after the rainy season has
ended.

**Agrimony** *Agrimonia eupatoria* (Liverwort, Stickwort)
(△ of △) △ of △ ♃ ♎ (♐ ♋ ♄ ♇)
Oil; medicinal; sachet.
Banishes negativity, reverses incantations.
Young shoots, leaves and flowers are harvested together
midsummer.

**All Heal** *see* **Valerian**

**Almond** *Amygdalus communis*
(△ of △) ▽ of △ ☉ ♌ (♃ ♀)          Woody Perennial
Incense mix; sachet mix; oil; perfume; wood; flower.
Almond in flower ♆ : clairvoyance; divination.
Bitter Almond Oil. (♀)

**Aloe** *Aloe Vera*
(△ of △) △ of △ ♂ ♎ (♈ ♐ ☉ ♇)          Perennial
Lignum Aloes perfume 4th, 11th and 28th lunar mansions.
Sachet mix; sacrificial burning; incense; perfume; balsam;
psychic correspondence; transmutation; talismatic.
Juice is extracted by bruising leaves; gum is taken by incision;
gum is usually mixed with myrrh.
Agreement in marriage and reconciliation. For love.
Guards against accidents, brings luck, protection.

## Amber
Fossil resin of extinct coniferous tree (Succinite) extinct. ♀
Perfume—4th lunar mansion; medicinal; amulet (worn by Roman women as protection from witches).

## Amaranth *Amaranthus hypochondriacus*
(▽ of ▽) ▽ of ▽ ♀ ♏ (♄ ♉)　　　　　　　　　　Annual
Symbol of Immortality; Athena; Uranus; for working of Holy Guardian Angel. Protection.

## Ambergris
(▽ of △) △ of △ ♆ ♈ (♇)
Formed in intestinal track of sperm whale.
Psychic correspondence; oil; perfume; works of wrath and vengeance; fixative.

## Angelica *Angelica archangelica*
(△ of △) △ of △ ☉ ♊ (♌ ♋)　　　　　　　　　　Biennial
Sachet mix; incense; dry use; perfume; angelica root oil; resin; medicinal; wine.
Liqueur defence against spirits; cures poison; keeps bad air away; attributed to Michael the Archangel.
Resinous gum gathered and used in Pot Pourri in place of musk; indoor garden magic and dry use—'when root is in house naught harm can come from demons'.
Gum taken by cut in stems and crown of root in spring. Root harvested after 2-3 years of growth.
"Angelica Incense" see page 78.

## Anise *Pimpinella anisum*
(△ of ▽) △ of ▽ ♂ ♋ (♅ ☿ ♃ ☽ ♌)　　　　　　Annual
Sachet mix; aromatic fatty oil; perfume; dry use; culinary; medicinal; cosmetic.
Liqueur; psychic work; philtre.
Outcasts possessive spirits. Relaxant.
Seeds collected when they turn grey brown, stems yellow when plant is ready.
– Star Anise oil.

**Apple** *Pyrus malus*
($\triangle$ of $\triangle$) $\triangle$ of $\triangle$ ♀ ♎          Fruit tree
Sachet mix; woodbase (tree); love charms; philtre.
Devils lure; enticing; temptation; indulgence; earthly desires; disobedience; loss of innocence.
Aid in entering underworld, symbol of immortality; love spells.

**Arnica** *Arnica montana* (Wolfsbane/Leopards bane)
($\triangle$ of $\triangle$) $\nabla$ of $\triangle$ ♂ ♌          Deciduous
Sachet mix; balsam; bath; (poisonous); blue aromatic oil; greenish yellow resin; medicinal.
Restricted dosage if taken internally.
In earthly desires.
Collect fully developed fresh flowers early summer. Roots collected after 2-3 years growth.

**Artemisia** *Artemisia dracunculus* (Tarragon)
($\nabla$ of $\nabla$) $\nabla$ of $\nabla$ ♆ ♍ (♀)          Perennial
Named from Dianna Artemis.
Potion for psychic dreams; talisman; oil; relaxant in psychic work; culinary; medicinal.
*Artemisia vulgaris* see **Mugwort**
*Artemisia abrotamum* see **Lads Love**
*Artemisia absinthium* see **Wormwood**

**Asafoetida** *Ferula foetida, F. rubicaulis*
($\triangle$ of $\triangle$) $\triangle$ of $\triangle$ ♅ ♊ (♄)
Dry use. For protection. Incense.

**Ash**
($\triangle$ of $\triangle$) $\triangle$ of $\triangle$ ☉ ♐ (♀ ♃)          Woody Perennial
Woodbase; wood; potion for psychic dreams.
Works concerning death.
Wands for healing are made from the wood; prosperity workings.

**Avens** *Geum rivale, Geum virginianum* (Star of the Earth)
♃
Dry use.
For protection against poisonous creatures; exorcism.

**Balm** *Melissa officinalis*
(△ of ▽) △ of ▽ ♃ ♋                    Woody Perennial
Balm Tree ♎
Sachet mix; dry use; medicinal; culinary; liqueur; perfume;
balsam; flower; potion; bath.
Calms nerves. Drives away melancholy and bad dreams.
Lemon Balm as a sprig worn around neck of woman makes
her beloved and faithful.
Fresh plants make balm oil.
Collect whole plant early spring when flowering commences.

**Barley** *Hordeum vulgare*
(▽ of ▽) △ of ▽ ☽ ♍                              Annual
Sachet mix; wiccan use.

**Basil** *Ocimum basilicum*
(△ of ▽) ▽ of ▽ ♂ ♏ (♇)                         Annual
Sachet mix; woodbase; perfumed oil; salve; dry use; amulet;
medicinal; culinary; potion.
Attracts money if carried in pocket (Mexico); draws poison;
stimulates sensuality; in Haiti associated with pagan goddess
of love; it is sprinkled to keep away evil spirits; to bring
prosperity; if wife dusts basil powder over top half of body her
husband is stopped from wandering and becomes faithful and
loving.
The scent stimulates and revives. Protection from water
demons.
Turns pale at the rising of the dog-star; pick in the autumn.
Collect whole plant while flowering.

**Bay Laural** *Laurus nobilis*
(▽ of △) △ of △ ☽ ♈ (☉ ♇) ♌         Evergreen
Clairvoyance; divination; sleep pillow; dry use; woodbase; wood; sacrificial; wet burning; dry burning; bay leaf oil; medicinal; culinary.
Wherever a bay tree is, there is protection. Sacred to Apollo and used in worship; confers gift of prophecy; chewed as drug to procure visions; leaves, berries and oils are narcotic; the incense is burned as an offering.
Place under a pillow and you will have pleasant dreams. Hang over doorway to keep away poltergeists. Plant for money and business.
Laurel leaves were chewed by the Priestesses of Delphi.
Used as protection; incense for heaving; for creative work.

**Bean** *Phaseolus vulgaris*
(△ of ▽) △ of ▽ ☉ ♍ (♏ ♀)         Annual
Sachet mix; dry use.
Fertility symbol. Regarded as deterrent against evil because a seed within it stores the positive life force of all living and growing things.

**Beech** *Fagus Spp.*
(▽ of △) △ of △ ♄ ♐         Woody Perennial
Sachet mix; wood.
The earth around the base was considered the underworld, the lower branches where people lived surrounded by a ring of water, and the upper branches the heaven.

**Belladonna** *Atropa belladonna* (Deadly nightshade)
(△ of ▽) △ of ▽ ♇ ♑ (♄)         Perennial
Drug; hallucinogenic (poisonous—restricted use); stimulant in small doses; medicinal.
Sorrow; of the Greek goddess of fate, Atropos.
Pick early morning when the atrophine content is high.

**Benzoin** *Styrax benzoin* (Gum Benjamin)
($\triangle$ of $\triangledown$) $\triangle$ of $\triangledown$ $\odot$ $\eightpointed$ ($\female$)          Woody Perennial
Wood; perfume; cosmetic; incense; psychic correspondence;
balsam; oil; sachet. Scent of essence in incantations, seances.
To Triumph. For love matters.
Gum obtained by incision.

**Bergamot** *Citrus aurantium*
($\triangle$ of $\triangle$) $\mercury$ $\gemini$
Small fruit bearing tree
Perfume oil from rind of fruit; sleep pillow.

**Betony** *Stachys officinalis*; *Betonica officinalis*
($\triangle$ of $\triangle$) $\triangle$ of $\triangle$ $\jupiter$ $\gemini$ ($\aries$)          Perennial
Aromatic oil; dry use and garden magic (indoors); potion.
Place the root in the house and no evil will come in; protection
from witchcraft.
Betony tea shields the dreamer from monstrous nocturnal
visitors, bad visions and dreams.
Wood betony as dry use, place under pillow to prevent
nightmares.
Whole plant is collected late summer.
*Betonica aquatica* $\jupiter$ $\cancer$ $\triangle$ of $\triangledown$

**Birch** *Betula alba, B. lenta*
($\triangledown$ of $\triangle$) $\triangle$ of $\triangle$ $\saturn$ $\sagittarius$ ($\female$)          Woody Perennial
Woodbase; wood; birch oil is 'oil of wintergreen'; potion.
Potion drunk at night ensures peaceful sleep. For exorcism.
To strike, punish; witches were said to ride on a birch
broomstick.

**Birds Tongue** *Fraxinus excelsior* (European Ash)
($\triangle$ of $\triangle$) $\triangle$ of $\triangle$ $\mars$ $\sagittarius$          Woody Perennial
Sacred in Northern Europe; represented the cosmos, roots are
underworld, the earth the middle land.

**Birthwort** *Aristolochia clematis* (Travellers Joy)
(△ of ▽) ▽ of ▽ ♅ ♏                          Woody Vine
To aid a speedy delivery/journey. Whole plant dug out in
third year.

**Bloodroot**
(▽ of ▽) ♄ ♑
Fresh and dry use—for protection.

**Blue Flag** *Iris versicolor*
(△ of ▽) △ of ▽ ♃ ♋                              Perennial
Sachet mix.

**Borage** *Borago officinalis*
(△ of △) ▽ of △ ♃ ♒ (☉ ♌ ♃)                     Annual
Culinary; medicinal; dry use; aromatic volatile oil.
For money and business; makes people merry, the mind glad;
for courage.
Collect leaves, flowers, stem by cutting stem but leaving
enough stem for second crop to come up.
(restricted dosage)

**Broomtops**
For protection, used in purified water and sprinkled—
aspurging.

**Bryony** (a) *Bryonia alba* (White Bryony, English Mandrake)
(△ of ▽) △ of ▽ ♇ ♍                     Perennial climber
Love potion; drug.

**Bryony** (b) *Bryonia diocia* (Red Bryony)
(△ of △) △ of △ ♂ ♊ (♇)                 Perennial climber
Sachet mix; drug.
Plant of trickery.

**Burdock** *Arctium lappa*
(△ of △) ▽ of △ ♃ ♌ (♀)
Dry use; medicinal.
For protection.
Collect root in second year of growth.

**Buttercup** *Ranunculus acris, R. bulbosus*
($\triangle$ of $\triangledown$) $\triangle$ of $\triangledown$ $\odot$ ♋            Perennial
Poisonous. Protection.

**Calamint** *Calamintha officinalis*
($\triangle$ of $\triangledown$) $\triangle$ of $\triangledown$ ☿ ♍
Helps a man keep a woman away. Help women prevent pregnancy. *Warning*—Too strong for most women.

**Calamus** *Acorus calamus* (Sweet Flag)
($\triangledown$ of $\triangledown$) $\triangle$ of $\triangledown$; ☿ ♍         Perennial
Essential oil; balsam.
Used by Moso Sorcerers of Yunnan and China—holy anointing oil, stimulant.

**Camomile** (a) *Anthemis nobilis*
($\triangle$ of $\triangle$) $\triangledown$ of $\triangle$ $\odot$ ♌          Perennial
Balsam; flower; oil; perfume; medicinal; cosmetic; the scent tranquilises; baths; potion (aids sleep).
Relaxant in psychic work, for mental steadiness in psychic work.
Potion for psychic dreams. Place under pillow to prevent nightmares.
(restricted dosage)

**Camomile** (b) *Matricaria chamomilla*
($\triangle$ of $\triangle$) $\triangledown$ of $\triangle$ $\odot$ ♌        Wild Annual
As above. Blue aromatic oil—oil has poisonous properties.
Collect flowers without calyx as long as plant blooms.

**Camphire** *Lawsonia alba, L. inermis* (Henna)
($\triangle$ of $\triangle$) $\triangledown$ of $\triangle$ ♂ ♌
Dye; spice and perfume.
Prized by the women of Egypt and by King Solomon.

**Camphor** *Cinnamomum camphora*
($\triangle$ of $\triangledown$) $\triangle$ of $\triangledown$ $\odot$ $\mathfrak{S}$                                                Tree
Perfume—1st lunar mansion; burned before Krishna.
Oil; balsam; perfume; wood; lessens sexual desire.
Distilled from chips of wood of root, trunk, branches, which
are exposed to the action of steam and afterwards refined.

**Cannabis** *Cannabis sativa* (Marijuana, Indian Hemp)
($\triangledown$ of $\triangle$) $\triangle$ of $\triangle$ $\Psi$ $\mathrm{I\!I}$                                    Annual
Hallucinogenic; fibre for rope, etc; medicinal.

**Carline Thistle** *Carlina acaulis*
($\triangle$ of $\triangledown$) $\triangledown$ of $\triangledown$ $\odot$ $\Upsilon$                                      Perennial
Aromatic oil; dry use.
A person carrying this thistle could draw strength into himself
from other people and animals. A man eating a cooked
Carline Thistle root could gain sexual strength and potency of
a stallion, but only if planting and harvesting is done properly.
Carrying the thistle protects one from harm.
Plant and harvest under new moon at stroke of midnight.
During growth fertilise with sperm of stallion if for sexual use
later. Roots collected in autumn of second year of growth.

**Carnation** *Dianthus caryophyllum*
($\triangle$ of $\triangle$) $\triangle$ of $\triangle$ $\female$ $\Libra$
Perfume; flower.
White—spiritual aspiration.
Red—to make things larger than life.

**Carraway** *Carum carvi*
($\triangle$ of $\triangledown$) $\triangle$ of $\triangledown$ $\mathfrak{P}$ $\mathfrak{S}$                                    Biennial
Sachet; culinary; medicinal; perfume; cosmetic; aromatic
green oil; wax.
Objects containing Carraway seeds cannot be stolen.
In operation and virtue to anise seed.
When in seed and seeds begin to darken, the plant is cut at the
base and hung over paper, which collects the seeds as they
fall.

**Cascarilla Bark** *Croton elutera*
($\triangle$ of $\triangledown$) $\triangledown$ of $\triangledown$ ☿ ♉ (♍)
Oil; incense.

**Cassia** *Cinnamomum cassia*
($\triangle$ of $\triangledown$) $\triangle$ of $\triangledown$ ☉ ♑ (♂)          Tree
Oil; wood; incense.
The bark is used as incense—aromatic. The scent is similar to
the Indian Orris Root. It is the Cedar of Lebanon, a symbol of
power and longevity.

**Catnip** *Nepeta cataria*
($\triangledown$ of $\triangledown$) $\triangle$ of $\triangledown$ ♀ ♋          Perennial
Incense; sachet; dry use.
Place around sleeping place for protection. Relaxant for
psychic work.
Propagation by division (self sowing).

**Cedar** *Cedrus libani*
($\triangle$ of $\triangle$) $\triangle$ of $\triangle$ ♃ ♐
Cedar Leaf Oil (Thuja Oil).
Perfume; oil; psychic correspondence; wood; woodbase; for
love; incense for money and business, also for psychic work.
For justice. Known in Lebanon as tree of power and longevity.
Cedar (white) *Thuja occidentalis*.

**Chervil** *Anthriscus cerefolium*
($\triangle$ of $\triangledown$) $\triangle$ of $\triangledown$ ♃ ♋          Annual
Sachet; culinary.
Harvest during flowering time or when seed is formed.

**Chicory** *Cichorium intybus* (Succory)
($\triangle$ of $\triangledown$) $\triangle$ of $\triangledown$ ♃ ♍ (☿)          Perennial
Sachet; talisman; amulet; aromatic oil; medicinal.
To win friendship of the noble, add a diamond for fame and
fortune.
Collect whole plant in flower and when stems are juicy.

**Cinnamon** *Cinnamomum zeylanicum*
(△ of △) △ of △ ⊙ ♈

Psychic correspondence; incense; oil of cinnamon obtained from inner bark and leaf.

Sexual stimulant to female upon inhalation—was used in Egypt for embalming and witchcraft; incense for creative work—money and business.

Oil of Cassia, as known in England.

**Cinquefoil** *Potentilla anserina* (5 Finger Grass)
(▽ of ▽) ▽ of ▽ ♀ ♉ (♃)                        Perennial grass

Balsam; love potion; sachet mix; talisman; amulet; increasing eloquence when seeking preferment; protection.

*Potentilla canadensis* and *Potentilla reptans*
(▽ of ▽) ▽ of ▽ ♀ ♉                        Perennial grass

*Potentilla tormentilla* (5 Fingered Grass)
(▽ of ▽) ▽ of ▽ ♄ ♉

**Civet** *Civettictus civetta; Viverra civetta*
(△ of ▽) △ of ▽ ♂ ♓                        Animal

Incense; erogenous added to bath; from member of cat family. Incense for psychic work.

**Clove** *Eugenia caryophyllus* or *E. c. aromaticus*
(△ of △) △ of △ ♀ ♈ (♃ ⊙)                        Evergreen tree

Aromatic; oil; psychic correspondence; sachet; aphrodisiac. Stills tongues; attracts riches.

**Clover**
(△ of △) △ of △ ♅ ♈                        Perennial

1-leaf clover stands for fame; 2 leaves for wealth; 3 leaves associated with Christian Trinity—the triad goddesses of the Greeks and Romans and sacred sun wheel of Celts, charm against witches, a faithful lover; 4 leaves ward off evil (symbol of cross), for good fortune, excellent health; 5-leaf clover is unlucky.

Red Clover—to dream of a field of clover is very fortunate. Relaxant in psychic work.

**Cocaine** *Erythroxylon coca*
(▽ of ▽) △ of ▽ ♅ ♓                                     Perennial
Hallucinogenic; dry use; sachet.
Invisibility; initiation; drug; Indians call it the divine plant of
the Incas; aphrodisiac.

**Coltsfoot** *Tussilago farfara*
(△ of ▽) ▽ of ▽ ☿ ♉ (♀)                                 Perennial
Sachet mix; volatile oil; potion; smoked.
For visions, peace.
Harvest leaves and rhizomes.

**Comfrey** *Symphytum officinale* (Salsify, Blackwort)
(▽ of ▽) △ of ▽ ♄ ♑                                     Perennial
Fixed star Algorab (♎ ♂ ♄)
Oil; medicinal; culinary; potion; cosmetic bath herb; health
food.
A daily drink of Comfrey, Alfalfa and Parsley mixed with fruit
juice is a marvellous tonic.
Oil taken from flower tops; collect roots early spring or late
autumn.

**Copal** *Copalquahuitl*
(▽ of ▽) △ of ▽ ♄ ♑
Gum; Mexican Copalli incense.

**Coriander** *Coriandrum sativum*
(△ of △) △ of △ ♂ ♈                                     Annual
Incense; sachet; oil; culinary; liqueur; medicinal (seeds); 1%
volatile oil, 13% fatty oil; the incense can infuriate the mind
for destructive purposes.
Love philtre to bind two people together.
Harvest when seeds turn yellow. Cut off at roots, lay in dry
spot to dry seeds.

**Corn**
(△ of ▽) △ of ▽ ☿ ♍ (⛢ ☉ ♉)                    Annual
Drug; oil.
Fertility rites; dry use.
Corn silk (*Stigmata maidis*) is the pistil of the corn plant.

**Cowslip** *Caltha palustris*
(▽ of ▽) ▽ of ▽ ♆ ♏ (♈ ♀)
Balsam; sedative; bath; medical.
Flowers in philtre.

**Cucumber** *Cucumis sativus*
(▽ of △) △ of △ ☽ ♎                             Creeping vine
Seed.
Incense; balsam.

**Cyclamen** *Cyclamen europaeum*
(△ of △) ▽ of △ ♀ ♌
Balm of Cyclamen; if potted in couple's bedroom, union will
be long and happy.

**Cypress**
(▽ of △) ▽ of △ ♄ ♒ (♇ ♀)
Perfumed oil; salve; scent tranquilises.
Incense in psychic work; brings justice.

**Daffodil** *Narcissus* spp.
(△ of △) ▽ of △ ☉ ♌ (♀) (Yellow ♂)
Love spells; fertility; luck.

**Daisy** *Chrysanthemum* spp.
(▽ of ▽) ▽ of ▽ ♀ ♉
Flower; balsam.
Purity, innocence and loyal love. Aphrodite, northern goddess
of love and spring, measure of love, good luck charm.
(restricted dosage)

**Dandelion** *Taraxaum officinale*
(▽ of △) △ of △ ♅ ♎ (♃ ♀ ☉ ♉ ♌)          Perennial
Sachet mix; potion; carries thoughts; to dream of a dandelion
is bad luck.
Relaxant in psychic work. Pharmacists use extract from
dandelion root as binder when making pills.
Harvest young leaves in spring, and root in third year of
growth.

**Dill** *Anethum graveolens*
(△ of ▽) △ of ▽ ☿ ♋ (♌)          Annual
Sachet; dry use; oil; perfume; medicinal; culinary; philtre.
Protection if placed in doorways and windows; effective
against negativity; provokes others to come to terms.
Cut stem when seed has ripened.

**Dittony of Crete** *see* **Oregano**

**Dock**—Water *Rumex hydrolapathum* (Bloodwort)
(▽ of ▽) △ of ▽ ♅ ♓ (♈ ♃ ♑)          Biennial
Medicinal. Good for business.

**Dragons Wort** *Polygonum bistorta* (Bistort)
(▽ of △) ▽ of △ ♄ ♒ (☿)
Fixed star Sirius (♋ ♃ ♂)
Sachet mix; incense mix; potion for divination and trance
work.

**Dragons Blood** *Daemonorops draco* in Indonesia; *Dracaena draco*
in Canary Isles
(△ of △) △ of △ ♂ ♈
Perfume (of aggression); incense; balsam; psychic correspondence; herb of torment (resin); works of wrath. Resin is
powdered.
Used in an incantation, to bring back a loved one.

**Elder** *Sambucus canadensis, S. nigra*
($\nabla$ of $\triangle$) $\triangle$ of $\triangle$ ♄ ♐ (♀)
Woodbase; wood; medicinal; amulet.
Beneficial medicinal qualities but considered evil and narcotic; to hide; transform self into a branch of an elder tree.
Berries are poisonous; they make fine amulets of protection.

**Ergot** *Claviceps purpurea* (a source of LSD. LSD-25)
($\nabla$ of $\nabla$) $\triangle$ of $\nabla$ ♆ ♓         Fungi; grows on Rye
Powerful hallucinogen; medicinal.
Can only be extracted for use through laboratory methods.
(restricted dosage)

**Eucalyptus** *Eucalyptus* spp. (Blue Gum Tree)
($\triangle$ of $\triangle$) $\triangle$ of $\triangle$ ☉ ♐ (♃)        Evergreen tree
Sachet; balsam; oil; wood; woodbase; sacrificial; wet burning; dry burning.
Incense for healing.
(restricted use)

**Fennel** *Foeniculum vulgare*
($\triangle$ of $\triangle$) $\nabla$ of $\triangle$ ☿ ♒ (♍ ♌ ☽)       Biennial
Fixed star Pleiades (♉)
Sachet; woodbase; culinary; medicinal; perfume; cosmetic; incense; potion; 10% fatty oil; bitter and sweet oil; volatile and aromatic.
Gives strength and courage; long life; (to sow—sorrow); an incense that can infuriate the mind for destructive purposes.
Fennel potion (with vervain), to fill another with desire.
Gives sight.
Cut stem when seed has ripened.

**Fern** female: *Polypodium vulgare*; male: *Dryopterus filixmas*
($\nabla$ of $\nabla$) $\nabla$ of $\nabla$ ♀ ♉        Female—perennial
($\triangle$ of $\nabla$) $\nabla$ of $\nabla$ ☿ ♉        Male—perennial
Sachet mix.
Male fern smoked and hung (as in smoking ham).

**Feverfew** *Chrysanthemum parthenium*; *Pyrethrum parthenium*
(△ of △) △ of △ ♇ ♈ (♐ ♀)
Protects against sickness, accidents and hysteria—medicinal for women.

**Fig Tree and Fruit** *Ficus carica*
(△ of ▽) △ of ▽ ♃ ♍ (♀)                          Perennial
Sachet mix; woodbase; perfume.
Perfumed flowers of fig tree 23rd lunar mansion.
For preservation of matters; power to attain ascendency; tree of heaven; phallus and fertility symbol.

**Flaxseed**
(△ of ▽) △ of ▽ ♂ ♑ (♄)                          Annual
Sachet mix.
For psychic powers; money and protection.

**Forget-me-nots**
(▽ of ▽) ▽ of ▽ ☽ ♉
For a lover parting on a journey.

**Foxglove** *Digitalis purpurea*
(△ of △) △ of △ ♀ ♎                               Biennial
Sachet mix.
Pick when plant is in bloom, the leaves are most potent at this time.
(restricted dosage)

**Frankincense** *Boswellia thurifera*
(△ of △) ▽ of △ ☉ ♒ (♌)                          Woody tree
Fixed star Pleiades (♉)
Perfume—13th lunar mansion.
Incense with works with any intent; psychic correspondence.
Talismatic. Brings justice; incense for healing.
    **Kyphi** Gum resin of tree (offered to Ra when sun set). Although foreign to the Greeks, they burned frankincense at bloody sacrifices both as offering to gods and as fumigation for evil odours. Burnt to Zeus, Meiluchios, Hermes, Sosipolis and Demeter.

**Olibanum** (☽ ♈) (☉) Balsam; incense; perfume; evocation.

**Galbanum**
(△ of △) ▽ of △ ♅ ♒ (☉ ☽ ♎) Incense; perfume; oil; divination; astrology.

**Garlic** *Allium sativum*
(△ of △) △ of △ ♂ ♈                                    Perennial
Oil; sachet; dry use; culinary; medicinal; potion.
Strength and nourishment; inspires courage; wards off vampirism; power against evil; protection.

**Geranium**
(▽ of ▽) △ of ▽ ♀ ♓
Oil; flower to aid in fight or to obtain one's desires.

**Ginger** *Zingiber officinale*
(△ of △) △ of △ ♂ ♈                                    Perennial
Oil; perfume; culinary; incense (martial); philtre.

**Ginseng** *Panax schin-seng, P. quinquefolius*
(△ of ▽) △ of ▽ ☉ ♍                                    Perennial
Balsam; psychic correspondence; sachet; incense; oil; philtre.
A link between man and unseen spiritual reality; plant contains an embodiment of the spirit of the universe; spirit of the earth.
Panacea (elixir of life)
For visualisation in psychic work. For divination, trance and creative work.

**Gota Cola**
(△ of ▽) ▽ of ▽ ☉ ♏
For visualisation in psychic work.

**Goutwort** *Aegopodium podagraria*
(▽ of ▽) △ of ▽ ♄ ♑                                    Perennial

**Grain of Paradise** *Aframomum melequeta*
($\triangle$ of $\triangle$) $\triangledown$ of $\triangle$ $\odot$ $\Omega$ ($\male$)
Philtre, incense.
Luck; money; wishing.

**Groundsel** *Senecio vulgaris*
($\triangle$ of $\triangle$) $\triangle$ of $\triangle$ $\female$ $\libra$
Amulet.
For health.

**Hawthorn** *Crataegus oxyacantha*
($\triangle$ of $\triangle$) $\triangle$ of $\triangle$ $\male$ $\sagittarius$      Woody Perennial
Woodbase.
White Hawthorne ($\female$) is regarded as the holy tree. To cut one down was to result in trouble from the supernatural. The scent is considered harmful when the flowers have been fertilised, for it gives an odour of decay.

**Heliotrope** *Heliotropium europeum, H. aborescens*
($\triangle$ of $\triangle$) $\triangledown$ of $\triangle$ $\odot$ $\Omega$
Incense; dry use.
To find stolen goods gather Heliotrope in February, then during sign of Leo wrap flowers in bay leaves with tooth of wolf and place under pillow at night; during sleep you will dream of where the goods are.

**Hellebore** black *Helleborus niger*; white *H. foetidus*; green *H. viridus*
($\triangle$ of $\triangle$) $\triangle$ of $\triangle$ $\pluto$ $\libra$ ($\saturn$)      Perennial
Black: poison; love potion; sachet mix; incense.
Fixed Star Algol ($\taurus$ $\saturn$ $\jupiter$)
Herb of torment; drug perfume of aggression.
White: poison, herb of torment; drug; sachet mix; incense; most active of the three.
Green: more potent than black and white Hellebore.

**Hemlock** *Tsuga canadensis* (Spruce)
(▽ of ▽) △ of ▽ ♄ ♅ (♂)                    Evergreen
Oil; incense; wood; talisman; sacrificial; dry use.
An incense which can infuriate the mind for destructive purposes. Olive leaves are added to Hemlock, which means that the destruction of enemies is achieved by more peaceful means.

**Hops** *Humulus lupulus*
△ of △ ♂ ♈                              Perennial vine
Relaxant in psychic work.

**Hemp** (Indian Hemp)
(▽ of △) △ of △ ♆ ♈ (♄ ♅)
*See* **Cannabis**: Hallucinogenic.
Hemp seed—love spell.

**Henbane** *Hyoscyamus niger*
△ of △ ♅ ♒ (♅ ♄)                        Biennial
Fixed star Algorab (♎ ♂ ♄)
Incense; dry use.
Poisonous.

**High Joan (John) The Conqueress** *Ipo-moea purga*; *I. jalapa*
(△ of △) ▽ of △ ☉ ♌
Oil; sachet; against depression and to destroy curses.
Protection; for money and business.

**Honeysuckle** *Lonicera periclymenum*
(▽ of △) △ of △ ☽ ♊ (♂ ♋)                Vine
Flower; perfume—for agile and versatile mind; oil.

**Horehound** *Marrubium vulgare* (White Horehound)
(△ of ▽) ▽ of ▽ ☿ ♏                      Perennial
Fixed star Capella (♊ ♂ ☿)
Medicinal; sacrificial; volatile oil.
Dedicated to Horus in earlier times.
Harvest mid-summer; collect only upper third of flowering branches.

**Horseradish** *Armoracia lapathifolia*
△ of △ ♂ ♈                                              Perennial
Volatile aromatic oil; resin; gum; starch.
Medicinal.
Harvest autumn of third year (whole plant), store as you
would potatoes.

**Horsetail** *Equisetum arvense*
(△ of △) △ of △ ♂ ♈ (♄)
Extracts.
Collect mid-summer, only upper part of stems.

**Houndstongue** *Cynoglossum officinale*
(△ of ▽) △ of ▽ ♂ ♍ (♋ ☿)                            Biennial
Put with heart of young frog and her matrice, and put them
where you wilt, and after a while all dogs in area will be
gathered around. If herb under foremost toe, the dogs remain
silent.

**Hyssop** *Hyssopus officinalis*
(△ of ▽) △ of ▽ (♃ ♋ (♂ ☽)                          Bushy evergreen
Sachet; medicinal; liqueurs; perfumes; domestic; aromatic oil;
fatty oil; bath.
Power of attaining ascendency; used in water for purification.
For protection.
Flowers and leaves are collected mid-summer.

**Iris** *Iris foetidissima* (Yellow flag, Gladwin)
(△ of △) ▽ of △ ♂ ♒                                  Perennial
Symbol of life and resurrection. Osiris and Horus.

**Ironwood**
(△ of △) ▽ of △ ♇ ♌ (♂)
Incense in psychic work.

**Ivy** *Hedera helix*
(▽ of ▽) ▽ of ▽ ♀ ♏ (♄)                              Perennial
Fixed star Alphecca (♏ ♀ ☿)
To bind something and fasten it; used as voodoo dolls; flowers
bound in garlands for divination.

**Jasmine** *Jasminum officinale*
(△ of ▽) △ of ▽ ☿ ♋ (♃ ♀ ♋)        Vine-like indigenous
Oil; perfume; incense; psychic correspondence; salve; sachet
mix; sleep pillow; for love matters.
Great visions, vision of machinery or universe. The scent
stimulates and revives. Tantrics anoint their hands with
Jasmine.

**Jimson Weed** *Datura stramonium* (Thorn Apple)
▽ of △ ♆ ♒
Hallucinogenic; pubity rites; aphrodisiac; aid to cast spells.
Gather in 7th and 8th moon.
(restricted dosage)

**Juniper** *Juniperus communis*
△ of △ ♂ ♈
Salve; perfumed oil; scent stimulates and revives; Juniper
berries as sachet mix; wine; philtre.
Prickly Juniper gives Cade Oil.

**Lads Love** *Artemisia abrotanum* (Southernwood)
△ of △ ☿ ♊        Perennial shrub-tree
Dry use; wet burning; aromatic oil; wax; wood.
Promotes hair growth; believed to help the dead to sleep;
helps sleep; bark is made into rope.
Berries are collected.

**Ladies Mantle** *Alchemilla vulgaris*
(△ of ▽) ▽ of ▽ ♅ ♏ (♀)        Perennial
Medicinal.
Whole plant collected when harvesting during blossoming
time.

**Lavender** *Lavendula vera*; *L. officinalis*
(△ of △) ▽ of △ ☿ ♌
Sachet; an aphrodisiac; perfume; smoked as in smoking ham;
cosmetic; flower; oil; dry use; medicinal; amulet; incense;
bath.
Chastity; love charm; combined with Rosemary as perfume to

calm and make wise; perfumed oil relieves depression; incense
for creative work; relaxant in psychic work; sleep pillow for
psychic work.
Gather lavender spikes in autumn and early morning after
dew has dried. For distillation of aromatic oil collect
unopened flowers early morning.

**Leek** *Allium porrum*
($\nabla$ of $\triangle$) $\triangle$ of $\triangle$ ♅ ♊ (♍)          Perennial
Dedicated to the Roman gods Jupiter and Thor.
Dissipates atmospheric electric charges; wards off lightning.

**Lemon** *Citrus limon*
($\triangle$ of $\triangle$) $\nabla$ of $\triangle$ ☉ ♌          Evergreen citrus
Perfume; oil; incense; dry burning; sacrificial; woodbase.

**Lettuce** *Lactuca sativa*
($\nabla$ of $\triangle$) $\nabla$ of $\triangle$ ☽ ♌          Annual
Wild lettuce (*Lactuca virosa*). Biennial. Dried and smoked like
opium—sedative.

**Lily of Valley** *Convallaria majalis*
($\nabla$ of $\nabla$) $\triangle$ of $\nabla$ ☽ ♓          Perennial
Incense; oil; balsam; represents eternal sleep.
The scent is considered precious.

**Lily** (Water Lily)
($\nabla$ of $\nabla$) $\nabla$ of $\nabla$ ☽ ♏          Perennial
Sachet; incense; anaphrodisiac qualities.
Virginal, immortality and fertility.
Yellow Lily ☽ ♓

**Lime** *Tilia europaea* (Lime Tree)
($\triangle$ of $\nabla$) $\nabla$ of $\nabla$ ☿ ♉ (♃)          Citrus Tree
Perfume; aromatic oil; incense; resin; bath; tea.

**Linden** *Tilia europaea* (Lime Tree Flowers)
($\triangle$ of $\nabla$) $\nabla$ of $\nabla$ ☿ ♉
Sleep pillow; relaxant; philtre; oil.
For psychic work.

**Lotus** (white) *Nymphaea lotus*
($\nabla$ of $\nabla$) $\triangle$ of $\nabla$ ☽ ♓
The great work; clairvoyance; talismans; incense.

**Lotus** (blue) *Nymphaea caerulea*
$\triangle$ of $\nabla$ ♃ ♓
Very sacred, spiritualist cult.

**Lotus (rose)** *Neleumbium speciosum*
($\triangle$ of $\nabla$) $\triangle$ of $\nabla$ ♂ ♓
The round leaves and spherical fruit of Lotus were symbolic of intellect, its coming up from the mud supremacy of mind over matter, intellectual sovereignty as the surface of the water. Sacred in India, Tibet, China and Egypt.

**Lotus (Yellow)** ☿ ♓

**Lovage** *Levisticum officinale*
($\nabla$ of $\nabla$) $\nabla$ of $\nabla$ ♀ ♉ (☉)                Perennial
Sachet; perfume; potion; medicinal; volatile oil.
Root is collected when one year old only.

**Lungwort** *Pulmonaria officinalis*; *Anchusa officinalis L.*
$\triangle$ of $\triangle$ ☿ ♊ (♃)                Perennial
Medicinal.
Harvested when plant in flower, mid-summer. Root collected in autumn; ground leaves are collected after flowering season.

**Mandrake** *Mandragora officinarum*
($\nabla$ of $\nabla$) $\nabla$ of $\nabla$ ♆ ♉ (♄ ☿ ♀ ♋)                Perennial
Fixed stars Deneb Algedi (♑ ♃ ♂), Spica (♎ ♂ ♀)
Sachet mix; emblem; talisman; dry use; incense.
Narcotic, mystic plant; fertility drug; love plant; good luck charms; capable of working any spell; root resembles whole of male body except head; inducer of sleep; pain killer; for psychic work; protection.
English Mandrake is White Bryony.
When pulling from ground, guard against hearing the plant scream. Pick when moon is waxing, just after new moon,

between winter solstice and vernal equinox at night. Loosen
earth around root, then draw root out without injuring plant.
Trim foliage off main stem, leave small piece of root adhering
to it. Replant small root in spot where main plant was drawn.

**Marjoram** *Majorana hortenis*
(△ of ▽) △ of ▽ ♅ ♏ (☿ ♈)                                    Perennial
Fixed star Deneb Algedi (♏ ♂ ♃)
Sachet; oil; balsam; perfume; medicinal; culinary; sleep bag;
domestic; philtre; scent tranquilises and brings peaceful sleep,
symbol of happiness.
For concentration and memory.
Collect leaves and stems before flowers appear.

**Marigold** *Calendula officinalis*
(△ of △) ▽ of △ ☉ ♌
Fixed star Procyon (♋ ☿ ♂)
Oil; flower; perfume; love charm in garden magic; medicinal;
dye.
If gathered when sun in Leo, and wrapped in Laurel leaf or
May tree leaf and a wolf's tooth added thereto, no man shall
be able to have one word to speak against the bearer thereof,
but words of peace. If anything is stolen, and the bearer of the
things before named, lay them under the head at night and a
vision of the thief is shown.
Place Marigold in church and unfaithful wives will not enter.

**Mastic** (Gum Mastic)
△ of △ ☉ ♊
Fixed Star Regulus (♂ ♃ ♌)
Fixative; sealant—24th and 28th lunar mansions.
For reconciliation; talismatic.

**Meadow Sweet** *Filipendula ulmaria*
(△ of △) △ of △ ♀ ♎ (♊ ♃)
Love magic; medicinal; to keep the peace.

**Milfoil** *Achillea millefolium L.* (Common Yarrow)
(△ of ▽) ▽ of ▽ ♂ ♏ ♊
Gum; resin; medicinal; dry use.
Held in hand removes fear and fantasy.
*See* **Yarrow**.

**Milk Thistle**
(△ of ▽) ▽ of ▽ ♂ ♉ (♀ ♃ ♌)
Fixed star Aldebaran.
Said to give riches and honour—dry use.

**Mint** *Mentha crispa* (curled mint); *Mentha spicata* (spearmint); *Mentha aquatica* (water mint)
(△ of △) △ of △ ☿ ♊ (♀ ♃ ♌)
Fixed star Capella (♊ ♂ ☿)
Sachet mix; aromatic oil; wet use; perfume; liqueur; potion; bath; balsam; medicinal; culinary; refreshes the spirits of man.
Relaxant in psychic work.
Daughter of the river god Cooyte, who was Mentha and was changed into Mint.

**Mistletoe** *Viscum album* (European Mistletoe)
(△ of △) ▽ of △ ☉ ♌ (♃)　　　　　　　　Evergreen
Sacred to Druids; love philtre with Vervain to make one desire you. Ensures good luck.
Mix with Martegon (Silphion or Laserpitium) and it opens locks.
Put mixture in mouth and all thoughts are created.

**Monkshood** *Aconitum napellus* (Wolfsbane)
(▽ of ▽) △ of ▽ ♄ ♑ (♇)　　　　　　　　Perennial
From Cerberus of the underworld; poison; numbs senses and gives sensation of flying.

**Moonwort**
(▽ of △) ▽ of △ ☽ ♒
Clairvoyance; divination.

**Morning Glory** *Ipomoea violacea* (seed known as Tlitliltzin)
($\nabla$ of $\triangle$) $\nabla$ of $\triangle$ ♉ ♌
Hallucinogenic, similar to LSD. Aztec priests used seeds with ashes of poisonous insects for tobacco, and some live insects as body-rub to make fearless. Mind alterant.

**Motherwort** *Leonurus cardiaca*
($\triangle$ of $\triangle$) $\nabla$ of $\triangle$ ♀ ♌                    Perennial
Power of prolonged life; protection; philtre.

**Mugwort** *Artemisia vulgaris*
($\triangle$ of $\nabla$) $\triangle$ of $\nabla$ ♇ ♋ (♀ ♄)                    Perennial
Fixed stars Capella (♊ ♂ ☿), Deneb Algedi (♑ ♂ ♃), Spica (♎ ♀ ♂), Algol (♉ ♃ ♄), Sirius (♋ ♃ ♂), Polaris (♊ ♄ ♀), Regulus (♌ ♂ ♃)
Tobacco substitute; dry use; sachet; dry burning; volatile oil; divination; incense; amulet; potion; domestic; medicinal; clairvoyance; repels insects; sleep pillow; protection against magic.
Place under doorstep and no annoying person will come to home; guards traveller against fatigue if worn; as a sleep pillow it procures dreams of future or unusual dreams; smoked as in smoking ham; dissolves weariness and he that bears it on his feet drives away venomous beasts and devils. Diana, artemis.
For visualisation in psychic work (teas for psychic dreams); for divination and trance work.
Gathered St John's Eve it makes fine amulet, or drink as a potion.
Flowers and leaves collected mid-summer. Root in autumn, the main root which is woody is discarded.

**Mullein** *Vebascum thapsus*
($\nabla$ of $\triangle$) $\triangle$ of $\triangle$ ♄ ♊                    Biennial
Dry use; philtre; medicinal; dye; protection against nightmares if hung over bed.
Overpowering effect on demons; used in incantations and

brews of love potions.
Yellow aromatic oil; yellow dye.
Flowers and leaves are collected.

**Musk** animal extract
($\nabla$ of $\nabla$) $\nabla$ of $\nabla$ ♀ ♏
Perfume—1st lunar mansion.
Aphrodisiac; incense; perfume; balsam; oil; arouses.
Tantrics anoint their vulva with musk.

**Mushroom** (Psilocybe)
$\nabla$ of $\nabla$ ☽ ♉ (♇ ♄ ♆)
Sachets; hallucinogenics; smoked.
Consumed in ritual.
Clairvoyance.

**Mustard** Black *Brassica nigra* White *B. hirta*
$\triangle$ of $\triangle$ Black ♂ ♈
$\triangle$ of $\triangle$ White ♂ ♎                           Annual
White mustard seed oil to illumine lamps.
Black mustard oil—lotion.

**Myrrh** *Balsomodendron myrrha* (Gum Myrrh tree)
$\triangle$ of $\triangle$ ☉ ♈ (♒ ♃)
Incense; balsam; fixative oil; perfumed oil; embalming;
compared to joys of sexual love.
Offered to Ra when sun at noon. Scent revives and stimulates.
Red Myrrh perfume—2nd lunar mansion.

**Nettle** *Urtica dioica*
$\triangle$ of $\triangle$ ♂ ♈                                Perennial
Vegetable drug; incense; dry use; fibre for rope and paper etc.
Hold in hand and be sure from all fear and fantasy or vision;
for binding of a spell.
Whole plant is collected in spring but rhizomes are collected
in autumn.

**Nightshade** *Solanum dulcamara*
($\nabla$ of $\triangle$) $\triangle$ of $\triangle$ ♄ ♎ (♅)          Perennial woody vine
Salve.
*Solanum nigrum* (Black Nightshade)
$\triangle$ of $\triangle$ ♅ ♎          Annual
Deadly poisonous.

**Nutmeg** *Myristica fragrans*
($\nabla$ of $\triangle$) $\triangle$ of $\triangle$ ☽ ♂ (♃ ♀)          Evergreen tree
Perfume—13th lunar mansion.
Oil—oil of nutmeg; incense for psychic work; for concentration and memory. Oil is rubbed on temples. Nutmeg is used for money and business.
A pain killer, mild hallucinogenic—can poison.

**Mace**
☿
Arillode of the Nutmeg. Incense for creative work; money and business.

**Oak**
Poison Oak ♄, English Oak ♄, red oak, white oak, black oak
$\triangle$ of $\triangle$ ☉ ♂ (♃)          Woody perennial
Incense; wood; sacrificial; wet burning; dry burning; wood; dry use; red dye.
Celtic—Druid.
Associated with thunder gods; tree of life; sacred to Zeus, Jupiter.
Connotes strength, masculinity, stability and longevity. Branch of oak over doorway affords protection.
Collect bark from young branches in spring. Acorns in autumn when they drop from tree.

**Olive** *Olea europaea*
($\triangle$ of $\nabla$) $\triangle$ of $\nabla$ ♃ ♋ (☉ ♌)          Evergreen
Sachet; oil; balsam; incense; woodbase; emblem; dry use; anointing for religious purposes; symbol of peace and wealth; for safe travel.

Greek goddess of wisdom, Athene—taught men to use the olive tree; to end a quarrel.
The oil is attributable to Minerva (goddess of wisdom), used to burn the temple lights.

## Onion
(△ of ▽) ▽ of ▽ ♂ ♉ (♄ ♈)                                    Biennial
Sachet mix.
Bulbs (fruit) were named and set beside a chimney, and the first to sprout named the future marriage partner.

## Oregano *Origanum vulgare* (Wild marjoram)
(△ of △) △ of △ ☿ ♊
Oil; medicinal; culinary; drives out venom and poison; potion. Gather when flowers show but have not opened; pick whole stalks and dry. Cut stalks away.

## Orris Root *Iris florentina* (Garden Iris, Yellow Flag)
(▽ of ▽) ▽ of ▽ ☽ ♉
Love root; sachet; oil; perfume; fixative.

## Parsley *Petroselinum sativum*
(△ of △) △ of △ ☿ ♎ (♌)                                     Biennial
Aromatic oil; fatty oil; ointment; balsam; medicinal; culinary; incense; perfume industry extracts an essential oil from the seed; domestic.
Triumph; the smoke of parsley drives away venomous beasts. Chief virtue is in the root; then seeds; the leaves least powerful. An ingredient in flying ointment; considered unlucky to transplant parsley from one home to another; was used in mourning by the Greeks.
Sow immediately after spring equinox. To nulify wickedness—sow on Good Friday under rising moon. Collect seeds before ripening by cutting umbells. Roots collected dried and ground make good incense.

**Parsnip**
△ of ▽ ☿ ♍ (♄)                                                    Annual
Sachet.

**Patchouli** *Pogostemon cablin; P. patchouli*
(▽ of ▽) △ of ▽ ♄ ♍
Perfume; oil and fixative as oil; exercises evil influence on moral characters.
Tantrics anoint their cheeks and breasts with Patchouli.

**Pennyroyal** *Hedeoma pulegioides*—annual; *Mentha pulegium*—perennial
(△ of ▽) ▽ of ▽ ♅ ♏ (♀)
Fixed star Procyon (♋ ♂ ☿)
Sachet; oil; dry use; wet burning; balsam; potion; sleep pillow; medicinal; domestic.
To make the speechless talk.
A garland of Pennyroyal made and worn about the head is of great force against swimming in the head and pains and giddiness thereof.

**Pepper**
White ♂ ♈ △ of △
Black ♂ ♈ △ of △
Oil.
For black pepper, gather berries while green and crush them. For white pepper, gather berries while ripe and turning red and crush them.

**Peppermint** *Mentha piperita*
(▽ of ▽) △ of ▽ ♀ ♋ (♒)                              Hybrid perennial
Oil; sachet; culinary; medicinal.

**Periwinkle** *Provinsa*
(△ of △) △ of △ ♀ ♊
Fixed Star Polaris (♊ ♀ ♄)
Love charm.

67

**Peyote** *Lophophora williamsii*
(▽ of △) ▽ of △ ♆ ♌ (♈)　　　　　　　　　Cacti
Fruit eaten.
Hallucinogenic; used in ritual practices; messenger of gods;
smoked.

**Pimpernel** *Pimpinella magna; P. saxifraga*
(▽ of ▽) ▽ of ▽ ♀ ♉
Medicinal; aromatic oil; benzoic acid; starch.
Collect roots in third year of growth.

**Pine** *Pinus* spp.; *P. pumilio*—dwarf
(△ of ▽) △ of ▽ ♇ ♑ (♂ ☿)　　　　　Evergreen
Oil; pine resin perfume—7th lunar mansion. Woodbase;
wood; dry use; fire worship; sacrificial; incense; medicinal.
Used when invoking Pan in matters sensual, evocative as it is
of woodland thickets and dark glades. Pine nuts in sachet use.
For psychic work. Justice.

**Pipiltzintzintli** *Salvia divinorum* (mint family)
(△ of ▽) △ of ▽ ♇ ♓
Hallucinogenic.

**Plantain** *Plantago lanceolata; P. major; P. media* (Lambs Tongue,
Ribwort)
(▽ of ▽) △ of ▽ ♄ ♑ (♂ ♀)　　　　　Perennial
Fixed star Arcturus (♎ ♃ ♂)
Dry use; sachet; sleep pillow; smoked as in smoking ham.
Well-trodden path of multitude that sought Christ.
Placed under pillow it repels bad dreams and spirits.
Leaves collected early spring.

**Poplar** *Populus tremuloides; P. candicans; P. balsamifera; P. nigra)*
(△ of △) △ of △ ♅ ♐ (♄)　　　　　Woody perennial
Wood; sacrificial; fire worship; balsam.

**Poppies** *Papaver rhoeas*
Oil                                                                     Biennial
Black: poison △ of ▽ ♇ ♂
Opium: (▽ of △) △ of △ ♆ ♈
Joy; tobacco type use. Drug (potent) narcotic; medicinal.
Pick early morning when morphine content is high in the
Opium poppy juice.
White: (▽ of △) △ of △ ☽ ♊

**Psyllium Seeds** *Plantago psyllium*
♄
Dry use; potion incense. To soften the stubborn. To see the
future.

**Pumpkin** *Cucurbita pepo*
(▽ of ▽) △ of ▽ ☽ ♋                                        Annual
Pumpkin seed oil illumines lamps.

**Purslane** *Portulaca sativa*
Sachet; dry use.
Protection.

**Rose** *Rosaceae* (Apothecary's Rose, Damask Rose, Old Cab-
bage Rose)
(▽ of △) △ of △ white ☽ ♎
(▽ of △) △ of △ roses ♀ ♎
(▽ of △) △ of △ yellow ☽ ♎
(△ of △) △ of △ red ♂ ♎
Perfume; sachet; oil; balsam; aromatic in general.
Strewn around area of work; for matters of love.
Activate vegetative life in man when combined with cross
(kundalini). Token of silence.
Yellow rose—perfect achievement.
White rose—purity.
Red rose—passion—in G.D. silencing of desires.
Rose water—used to perfume baths and anoint hands, etc.
The scent tranquilizes—used in love magic.

**Rosemary** *Rosmarinus officinalis*
(▽ of ▽) △ of ▽ ☽ ♋ (☉ ♃ ♎)                    Evergreen shrub
Fixed star Alphecca (♏ ♀ ☿)
Sachet mix; incense; garden magic; balsam; bath use; oil; dry use; wet burning; dry burning; perfume; potion.
For concentration and memory in psychic work; for mental steadiness in psychic work; prevents nightmares if placed under pillow.
Love philtre; absorbs negativity from people while growing.
Emblem of love; floral perfume; tobacco substitute; brings good luck and a powerful force against magic.
Romans believed it had the power to preserve bodies of the dead from corruption, and it was planted and strewn in and around the tombs. Rosemary has an evocative quality of supernatural intensity; uplifting quality. The scent brings memories back. The scented oil relieves depression.
When the root is in the house no harm will come from demons; hang over bed to prevent nightmares; scent preserves youth.
Worn as garland in Greece and Rome. The oil is used in the Greek Orthodox Church.
The root differs very little from the scent of frankincense.
Worn at weddings as omen of happy marriage.

**Rowan** *Sorbus aucuparia*
(△ of △) △ of △ ☉ ♂                    Deciduous or Shrub
Especially strong against psychic forces.

**Rue** *Ruta graveolens*
(△ of △) ▽ of △ ☉ ♌ (♄)                    Perennial
Medicinal; amulet; potion; dry use; cosmetic; sachet; aromatic oil.
'Herb of Grace'; repentance; protection against evil; sacrificial; herb of torment—it was thought that this herb could be used to torment others.
The seed taken in wine is an antidote against poisons.
Romans believed Rue gave second sight and their chiefs wore

chaplets of Rue. Arrows were rubbed with Rue, in the belief that they would always find their mark.

**Saffron** *Crocus sativus*
($\triangle$ of $\triangle$) $\triangledown$ of $\triangle$ $\odot$ $\Omega$ ($\jupiter$)          Perennial
Fixed star Antares ($\mars$ $\sagittarius$ $\jupiter$)
Saffron perfume—9th Lunar mansion.
Incense in psychic work; for divination and trance work as potion or incense; aids women's diseases; oil; yellow dye; culinary; medicinal; dry use; aromatic.
The plant is considered very valuable because only the stigma is used. It gives an aromatic odour. Dried Marigold petals can be a substitute.

**Sage** *Salvia officinalis*
($\triangle$ of $\triangledown$) $\triangledown$ of $\triangledown$ $\uranus$ $\taurus$ ($\jupiter$)          Perennial
Fixed star Spica ($\venus$ $\mars$ $\libra$)
Sachet; potion; garden magic; tobacco substitute; culinary; medicinal; perfume; Dalmation sage oil; fixative.
Taken as potion to promote longevity; immortality. It reflects fortune of man if flourishes in garden. Quickens the senses and memory, strengthens sinews.
Relaxant for psychic work and for concentration and memory.

**Clary Sage** *Salvia sclarea*
($\triangle$ of $\triangledown$) $\triangledown$ of $\triangledown$ $\uranus$ $\taurus$ ($\moon$)          Biennial
Clary Sage oil (a fixative).
Aromatic (restricted dosage).
Pick during Balsamic phase. Can be propagated by layering or cuttings.

**Sandalwood** *Santalum album*
($\triangle$ of $\triangledown$) $\triangle$ of $\triangledown$ $\virgo$ White $\mercury$, Red $\venus$ ($\sagittarius$ $\moon$)          Tree
Incense; sacrificial; perfumed oil; wood; clairvoyance; psychic correspondence; balsam.
Wood for temples and funeral pyres, oil which is also used as perfume. Scent stimulates and revives.
Brings justice—incense heals.

71

**St John's Wort** *Hypericum perforatum*
($\nabla$ of $\triangle$) $\nabla$ of $\triangle$ ♄ ♒ ($\Omega$ $\odot$)          Shrubby perennial
Oil; dry use; incense; smoked as in smoking ham; wet
burning; dry burning; amulet.
Purifying incense; assaults powers of evil; worn around neck
as protective amulet. Place at entrance for protection. Used
for invisibility—money and business.

**Savory** *Satureja hortensis*
($\triangle$ of $\triangle$) $\triangle$ of $\triangle$ ☿ ♊          Annual
Sachet; culinary; medicinal.
Relaxant in psychic work.

**Skullcap** *Scutellaria lateriflora* (Maddogweed)
($\nabla$ of $\triangle$) $\triangle$ of $\triangle$ ♆ ♈ (♍)          Indigenous
For visualisation in psychic work; potion for psychic dreams.
Tranquilizer; if smoked is similar to Marijuana. Potion in
Tantric work.

**Solomon's Seal** *Polygonatum multiflorum*
($\nabla$ of $\nabla$) $\triangle$ of $\nabla$ ♄ ♑          Perennial
Leaf like a pentagram, key to many things according to folk
lore; used in exorcism.

**Sorrel** *Rumex acetosa*
($\nabla$ of $\nabla$) $\nabla$ of $\nabla$ ☽ ♉ (♀)          Perennial
Incense; medicinal.

**Storax (Stacte)** *Liquidambar orientalis* (Oriental Sweet Gum)
($\triangle$ of $\nabla$) $\triangle$ of $\nabla$ ♀ ♓ (♏ $\odot$)
Liquid Storax—2nd, 17th, 25th and 27th Lunar mansions.
Perfume; incense.
Gum that distils from Myrrh. One of the ingredients that
burns on the golden altar of incense. Incense for creative work
and money and business.
For revenge, separation, enmity—ill will—for birth—or destruction.

**Strawberry** *Euonymus americanus; Fragaria vesca*
(△ of △) △ of △ ♀ ♎                                    Perennial
Medicinal; culinary; dry use.
Sensuality; earthly desires; amatory magic; make the heart
merry; potion.
Young leaves combined with Thyme make an excellent tea.
The fruit of strawberry was symbolised as the fruit of
righteousness.
Collect leaves early summer without the stalks. Berries ripen
mid summer.

**Succory** *see* **Chicory**
(△ of ▽) △ of ▽ ♃ ♍
Fixed stars Polaris (♀ ♊ ♄), Wega (♀ ♄ ☿)

**Sunflower**
(△ of △) ▽ of △ ☉ ♌                                   Annual
Sunflower seed oil, to illumine lamps; medicinal; culinary.
For matters of money and business.

**Tansy** *Tanacetum vulgare*
(▽ of △) △ of △ ♄ ♎ (♀ ♃ ☿ ♊)                        Perennial
Volatile aromatic oil; wax; medicinal; culinary; cosmetic;
liqueur; dye; embalming—preservative; immortality; for matters of love.
The crushed leaves produce green dye, flowers yellow dye.
Young shoots with leaves and flowers are collected early
summer, seeds collected in autumn.

**Tarragon** *Artemisia dracunculus*
(▽ of ▽) ▽ of ▽ ♆ ♏ (♂ ♈)
Talisman; culinary.
Relaxant in psychic work.

**Teasel, Wild** *Virgo pastoris*
(△ of △) △ of △ ♀ ♎
Take herb and temper with juice of Mandrake and give it to a
bird or any other beast—it brings forth birth.

**Thorn Apple** *see* **Jimson Weed**
▽ of △ ♆ ♒ (♃)
Hallucinogenic—gives illusion of flying; smoked.

**Thyme** *Thymus vulgaris* (Lemon Thyme)
(△ of △) △ of △ ☿ ♊ (♀)
Sachet; dry use; dry burning; wet burning; incense; sleep pillow; medicinal; culinary; domestic; potion; embalms and preserves; for courage; fumigant.
The sleep pillow is recommended for people with melancholy or epilepsy and nightmares. Livens spirits. Hang over bed to protect from nightmares. Relaxant in psychic work.
Fresh leaves are a source of oil of Thyme.
Harvest during flowering time.

**Tobacco**
(▽ of △) △ of △ ♄ ♎ (♂)
Perfume; incense; smoked.
The American Indian regarded tobacco weed to have supernatural powers and used it in ritual fumigation.
An incense in psychic work.

**Tragacanth** *Astralagus gummifer*
Fixative; incense base.

**Unicorn Root**
Used for protection.

**Valerian** *Valeriana officinalis*
(△ of ▽) ▽ of ▽ ☿ ♏ (♍)                          Perennial
Philtre.
Valerian sleep pillow as relaxant in psychic work.
For matters of love, money and business.
Valerian root volatile oil is used as massage oil for visualization.

**Verbena** *Lippia citriodora* (Lemon)
(△ of ▽) △ of ▽ ☿ ♓ (♀)
Oil; perfume; philtre.
Visualization.

**Vervain** *Verbena officinalis*
(▽ of △) △ of △ ♄ ♊ (♀)
Perfumed oil; balsam; incense; sachet; love philtre—potion;
amulet; smoked as in smoked fish.
Magical protection, holy food to produce magical spells.
Scent arouses. Love philtre with mistletoe to stir another's
heart. Love charm as oil; symbol of peace—to end a quarrel.
Place at doors and windows for protection. Relaxant in
psychic work.
Collect when sun and moon are *not* seen in sky. Replace with
honeycombs as recompense to earth. Gather with left hand at
rise of the dog star.

**Violet** *Viola odorata*
(△ of ▽) △ of ▽ ♃ ♋ (♀ ♎)
Flower; perfume; sachet mix; sleep pillow; incense; potion;
aromatic oil; bath; medicinal.
Beauty and transitory qualities of life; modesty and simplicity;
to soften nature; comfort; to aid peaceful sleep; it is unlucky to
take a single violet into a house. For matters of love.
Collect tops of plants by cutting them when flowering begins.

**Walnut** *Juglans nigra*; *J. cinerea*; *J. regia*
(△ of △) ▽ of △ ☉ ♌ (☿ ♊)                                    Tree
Wood; woodbase; culinary.

**Willow** *Salix alba*; *S. purpurea*; *S. nigra*; *S. caprea*
(▽ of ▽) △ of ▽ ☽ ♓                                           Tree
Woodbase; wood; amulet.
Western—mourning, unlucky love.
Eastern—associated with springtime, regeneration, eternal
friendship.
Used in love charm.
Collect bark from 2-4 year-old trees early in spring.

**Wintergreen** *Gaultheria procumbens*
(▽ of ▽̄) ▽ of ▽̄ ☽ ♉ (♄)                           Evergreen shrub
Oil; incense.
Sharpening the senses.

**Witchhazel** *Hamamelis virginiana*

($\triangle$ of $\triangledown$) $\triangle$ of $\triangledown$ $\sigma$ $\zeta$ ($\triangle$)                    Shrub or tree
Diviner's rod.

**Wormwood** *Artemisia absinthium*

($\triangle$ of $\triangledown$) $\triangle$ of $\triangledown$ $\mathsf{P}$ $\mathfrak{S}$ ($\sigma$ $\mathfrak{M}$)          Silky perennial
Balsam; dry use; divination; medicinal; liqueur; domestic; sleep pillow; incense; aromatic oil; yellow dye; smoked; absinthe.

Deprives man of courage; salve drives goblins away; ingredient of drink absinthe which deteriorates the nervous system and causes attacks similar to epileptic seizures. This herb can poison waters; steeped in wine it counteracts the effects of alcohol.

Wormwood placed on a cone of black paper connects one with the recently dead. For workings of wrath and revenge. Dream inducement. The scent makes the sick sleep. It is also an incense in psychic work. The incense is also burned on Hallowe'en to enable one to see the returning spirits of the mighty dead.

Leaves are collected twice a month.

There is a star called wormwood which fell from heaven at the sounding of the third angel.

**Yarrow** *see* **Milfoil**

$\triangle$ of $\triangle$ $\varphi$ $\Omega$

There are of course a great many more herbs unlisted here, but these herbs have not been forgotten and the readers may do their own research.

# CHAPTER SIX
# THE PRODUCT

One of the main problems associated with herbal combinations to employ in magic is the actual application of herbs and their associations. For example, if one wishes to use a magical influence such as love, one must give a definite aspect to that love and then associate it with the plant. This is quite a simple procedure if you use astrology as a common base. Therefore, if we wish to use the magical properties of a herb to attract love between a man and a woman (passion), we must look at the herbs under Venus, Mars and Libra. Some magical manuscripts when promoting love between the sexes have generalised love on a common basis, but with the intervention of modern astrology and the additional planets, we can now be more specific and very exact in relating a herb to a purpose, magical or otherwise. For example, brotherly love is under Uranus, spiritual love is under Neptune. Some of the remedies below may contradict with earlier herbal writings of medieval Europe, but the whole basis of this chapter is for specifics and not generalisations. What recipes are included in this chapter are given only as examples and guidelines to the methods of making the products.

In any magical work such as divination, talismatic consecration and even curses and spells, the operator must be very exact in what he requires the magical force to do. He should think very clearly of the *purpose*, analyse *by association* the herb needed, utilise the *correct astrological time* for picking and using, then utilise the herb for the purpose desired. The whole aspect is a very analytical one, with very little time or place for rather vague associations to plants and herbs.

## Incense

**Cones:** Take dried, powdered herb or herbs, add chosen oil or oils, and enough gum tragacanth to give a fairly stiff paste. Form into cones and dry in a warm place. (A mixture left to stand overnight 'takes' better. Be sparing with oils.)

**Pebbles:** Mix herbs of your choice with oil of your choice, and white of an egg.

### Other ways:

(a) Herb(s) powdered with oil of choice, plus gum benzoin as fixative and 1 oz potassium nitrate. (This is dropped on charcoal after storage, but if mixture is right a lit match only need be put to the mixture.)

(b) Just mix the powdered herb(s) and oil (store a long time before using—30 days).

(c) Winter incense (see recipe) works well when placed on a heater-top in a brass or metal dish. The scent will drift through the house as long as the heater is on.

(d) Light Bulb Incense: place asbestos ring around light bulb, then put a few drops of perfumed oil or perfume in the ring, turn light on.

(e) Pastilles are also burnt as incense. See recipe.

### Examples

For Love: mix dried, powdered Rose petals, Vervain, Wormwood, Pine and/or any other herb associated with love; mix with Rose oil or oil of Thyme and white of egg.

To clear a house of bad air and spirits—'Angelica Incense': Take root of Angelica, dry it in oven or before fire, bruise it well and infuse it 4-5 days in white wine vinegar. To make use of it, heat brick red-hot, lay Angelica root on brick.

# THE PRODUCT

Coloured incense:
Blue: compounded Roses and Violets
Purple: compounded Saffron, Cinnamon and Red Sanders
Scarlet: compounded Balm, Ambergris, Grains of Paradise, Saffron
Green: compounded Benzoin, Mace and Storax
White: compounded Camphor, Amber, Aloes, White Sandalwood, Cucumber seeds

Incense to see future events: To equal mix of Frankincense incense (below) add Pipiltzintzintli, magic Mushrooms, a bit of Parsley root. Pound together.

Brain Incense (to see future): Psyllium seeds, Violet and/or Parsley roots, Fleawort seeds, Henbane and Hempseeds.

Frankincense Incense:
1 oz each of powdered Frankincense, Benzoin, Orris Root.
½ oz each of ground Cascarilla Bark, Lavender, Cinnamon, Rose Petals and rasped Santal.
Mix together, add the following oils: Lemon, Clove, Patchouli.
Mix and store for a while before using.

An Egyptian version of Frankincense—Kyphi ingredients: Honey, Wind, Raisins, Sweet rush, Thyron, Dock, both kinds of Arcoutheld, Caramum and Orris Root.

Jewish ingredients: Pure Frankincense, Stacte, Onycha, Gallabanum.

Winter Incense:
1 part each of Lavender Buds, Clove, Cinnamon.
1⅓ part each of powdered Orris Root, Storax.
⅛ part each of the following oils: Lemon, Lavender, Clove, Bergamot.
Mix together and store.

79

Sandalwood Incense:
10 drops of Sandalwood oil dropped onto 4 oz rasped Santal.
2 oz each of gum Benzoin or Storax, ground Cascarilla Bark.
1 oz Potassium Nitrate
½ oz Balsam of Tolu
Add 10 more drops Sandalwood and add powdered Sandalwood to get consistency, mix smooth, store.
*Note:* oils are mixed separately from the herbs, then both herbs and oils are combined. Storage must be for 30 days or more.

## Pastilles

These do not harden and must be stored in airtight containers.

Pastilles of Myrrh:
2½ oz each of coarsely powdered Myrrh and Charcoal
½ oz each of coarsely powdered Cascarilla bark, Benzoin, and Storax.
Mix the above ingredients.
1 oz Potassium Nitrate, powdered Myrrh and 10 drops oil of Myrrh, 1 tsp gum Tragacanth with ¾ cup water stirred into a glue substance. Put all mixtures in top of double boiler, adding mucilage of Tragacanth slowly, making a thick paste. When heated until warm, remove from heat and mould the mixture into pastilles.

Rose Pastilles (for burning):
Grind the following separately: 3 oz Benzoin, 2 oz Storax, 1 oz Damask Rose Buds, ¾ lb each of Aloes, Amber, fine sugar, Civet, Cypress. Mix together with Gum Tragacanth that was dissolved in Orange flowers or Rose water.

The following mixtures are prepared in the hours and on the days given for the 'Incenses of the Seven Planets'. Potassium Nitrate is added to aid igniting.

*Sun*
Aloeswood, Cinnamon, Frankincense, Benzoin, oil of Cloves, Myrrh, Olibanum, Saffron.

*Moon*
Camphor oil, Rose, Honeysuckle, Rosemary, Olibanum, Lily of the Valley root and flower, Cucumber seeds, Orris Root.

*Mercury*
Marjoram, oil of Thyme, White Sandalwood, Caraway, Lavender, Parsley root, Styrax liquid, Storax, oil of Cloves.

*Venus*
Clove, Thyme, Red Sandalwood, Benzoin/Storax, Rose, Rose oil or Musk oil, Apple.

*Mars*
Benzoin, Coriander, Mustard, Nettle, Dragon's Blood, Witch-hazel oil, oil of Pine.

*Jupiter*
Cedar, Rosemary, Figwood, Storax/Benzoin, Ash, Olive oil, Violet.

*Saturn*
Wintergreen oil, Birchwood, Copal, Mandrake (preferably male), Cypress, Galbanum/Benzoin, Mullein oil/Patchouli oil, Vervain.

*Uranus*
Clover, Galbanum, Henbane, Asafoetida, Anise, Cornflower oil, Tragacanth.

*Neptune*
Ambergris, Bay Laurel, Cannabis/Hemp, Artemisia, Tragacanth, Ambergris oil.

*Pluto*
Basil, Mugwort, Pine, oil of Pine, Hellebore, Tragacanth (Sage oil), Wormwood.

### Balsams (salves and ointments)
In earlier times lard was used as a base for balsam, then salt-free butter, but now vaseline or petroleum jelly is used, and even cold cream.

The herb part is prepared, either dried and powdered or fresh and crushed with juice extracted. Then placed in a heating pot with the vaseline, or suchlike, melted at a low heat, brought to boil, stirred, taken off the heat, sifted through gauze or a dish-towel, pressing out the residue. Leave to cool and bottle the final product.

### Examples

Usually 1 or 2 heaped tablespoons of herb or herbs to 7 oz of vaseline, or suchlike.

Marigold Salve: 1 handful (2 oz) freshly picked Marigold flowers to 7 oz vaseline or other petroleum jelly. Melt vaseline in a pot over low heat, add Marigold flowers, bring the mixture just to the boil. Stir well. Sift through a dish-towel, pressing out the residue. Leave to cool.

Flying Ointment: Fat of an animal, simmer in juice of Stramonium, water Parsnip, Arconite, Cinquefoil and deadly Nightshade, strain and cool. My opinion of flying ointment is that it aids one to skry or fly out-of-body, rather than fly physically.

Sabbat anointing oil: Wild Parsley root, Celery root, Poplar leaves (Balm of Gilead), Cinquefoil, Saffron. Herbs are cut when moon is waxing, steeped and crushed in pure vegetable oil during waxing moon.

### Anointing:

Before anointing with balsam or oil, the hands should be well washed, preferably with Hyssop: Hyssop plus 1 pint hot water. Stand infusion for 15 minutes; or, the hands are perfumed with high-quality soap and water—then perfume-oiled afterwards.

Process of anointing.
Process 1:
♈ Head (top)
♉ Forehead with index finger between eyebrows
♊ Hands
♋ Breasts
♌ Chest
♏ Generative organs
♓ Feet

Process 2:
♈ Forehead (as before)
♉ Neck (back of neck)
♊ Arms and hands (back of hands)
♋ Stomach
♌ Upper spine
♍ Bowels (upper) e.g. belly button
♎ Lower lumbar region
♏ Lower bowel e.g. genital region
♐ Thighs
♑ Knees
♒ Ankles
♓ Feet

3 ingredients which were considered vital to all magic rites were Myrtle, Cinnamon and Olive oil.

**Juice**
is extracted by bruising leaves.

**Resin & Gum**
is taken by incision in bark.

**Oils**
Soak at least 10 successive batches of fresh petals in Olive, Safflower or Ben oil (or an oil of your choice providing

it is of a plant), leaving each batch in the oil for a day or two. When finished, strain plant out of oil and seal oil in brown bottle or jar.

Leaves or flowers can be used in the above method to extract the herb's essential oil. Crushing or bruising helps, and regular mixing.

To make an Attar of a herb, lightly press the herb down in a ceramic crock and cover with pure spring water or rain water. Place in a warm area or in the sun for a full day. A scum should form over a period of days which is the 'Attar' oil. With a piece of cotton absorb oil and squeeze it into a vessel. Do this daily.

The Laboratory method—herbal alchemy—is to use the distillation train, which will be explained in Chapter 7.

Steam distillations extract perfumes and essences and volatile oils.

In making infusions, the volatile oils are usually lost through evaporation. One way to prevent these volatile oils from escaping (for example, like the Thymol in Thyme) is to make the infusion inside a large vacuum flask with the lid sealed. The herbs are placed into a little metal basket, or on a mesh hung inside the flask near the top and above the boiling water. The oils are drawn out by the steam. This method is advantageous in that the plant can be withdrawn without sullying the liquid.

'Essential oils', which are the actual volatile oil of the herb extracted in the laboratory, should *not* be taken internally.

### Examples
Oil of St John's (Joan's) Wort: Crush 4 oz fresh, just-opened blossoms in approx 1 tsp Olive oil.
Pour 1 pint of Olive oil over whole and mix well.
Place in clear glass container, leave standing uncovered in warm spot to ferment 3-5 days.
After fermentation, seal container.
Place container in sun for 6 weeks until oil becomes bright red.

Press through cloth and pour off watery layer.
Keep well-sealed in dark-coloured bottle.
Taken internally the oil can relieve stomach pains. Externally, the oil relieves pain and helps heal burns and wounds.

Lavender Oil: Mix 1 part Lavender oil to 3 parts Olive oil, or 1 part Lavender oil to 1 part Coconut oil.

Rosemary Oil: Method 1: use of distillation train extracting oil (see Chapter 7).
Method 2: Place dried or fresh Rosemary leaves and flowers—crushed—into Olive or any other flower oil. Place in warm spot and allow to ferment for 3 days. Seal container and place in sun for 6 weeks. Strain solid matter out and seal oil in dark coloured bottle.

Witches Anointing Oil: Vervain, or Mint crushed and steeped in Olive oil or lard, left overnight, then squeezed through a cloth to remove leaves. This is repeated 3-4 times until balsam is strongly scented.

### Potions
Potions are made by pouring water over dried fresh herbs, then after a three-hour wait with occasional stirring, the mixture is strained and the juice extract drunk as a tea.

### *Example*
Memory Tea: 2 cups boiling water, add 1 tsp Rosemary and 1 tsp Sage. Steep 5 minutes, strain and drink daily for some time.

### Philtres (Tinctures)
The herb is crushed and steeped in boiling water or 70% proof or stronger alcohol, one part herb to 2 parts liquid. For water, the philtre must be used immediately to prevent bacteria from forming. With alcohol, the herb is left for several

days; then the herb is strained out of the liquid. Liquid is bottled. The alcohol philtre can be kept refrigerated for a month but it weakens with time.

### Example

To stir the heart of a loved one: Grind 7 Coriander seeds, naming intent 3 times. Add to ¼ cup boiling water. Add this to food or drink of intended within a couple of hours of making.

### Baths

There are, to my knowledge, six different methods of bathing with herbs. In all of the following cases, before bathing with the herbs wash excess dirt off self.

(1)   Simmer ½-1 cup herb(s) in 1 quart water, non-metal pot, for 10-20 minutes. Strain simmered herb(s) and pour herb liquid into bath. Wrap solid residue in washcloth and tie. Soak in bath 20 minutes or more, then rub body vigorously with herb washcloth.

(2)   Place herb(s) in bath and run hot water. Bathe after bath has cooled sufficiently.

(3)   Place a handful of herb(s) in 2 cups boiling water (non-metal container) and simmer for 10-20 minutes. Strain and wrap the solid matter in washcloth. Rub the body vigorously, then use the liquid to rinse.

(4)   Wrap herbs in cloth bag, and hanging this bag from tap or shower nozzle, run bath or shower.

(5)   Vapour method. Mix Coconut, Olive or Almond oil with water in electric frying pan or vapouriser with scented herb(s). e.g. Roses, Bay Leaves, Eucalyptus, Lemongrass, Lavender. Keep room sealed and let room steam up. Remain 20 minutes or more.

(6) As a bath oil, added to the bath. A few drops of essential oil of herb added to Babies' Oil, then added in small portion to bath—1 tsp.

### Sleep Pillows
Soft, porous cloth material is sewn into a small pillow and filled with dried, crumbled, scented herb(s).

### *Sachets:*
are a smaller version of sleep pillows.

### *Examples*
Dream Pillow: Mugwort pillow—8 oz Mugwort (dried) stuffed into a sewn pillow.

Anise Seed Sachet: Keep a small sachet of Anise seed in your pillow to aid a restful sleep. Keeps one from dreaming.

Love sachet aids woman in catching her man: Violet, Orris Root, Rose leaf, Rose petal, Tonka Bean.

### Sprinklers
Herbs gathered during carefully planned times according to the nature of the herbs. Bound together with thread specially spun or prepared for the operation. Place in sprinkler of rainwater and sea salt. Consecrate. After this you may use water sprinkler wheresoever you choose, and all negativity is chased away.

### Example from *Key of Solomon*. Sprinkler of Ver-
vain, Fennel, Lavender, Sage, Valerian, Mint, Garden Basil, Rosemary, and Hyssop gathered in the day and hour of Mercury, the Moon being in her increase. Bind these herbs with a thread spun by a young maiden, and engrave upon the handle on the one side the characters . . . . and on the other side those given in . . . . .

After this thou mayest use the water, using the sprinkler wheresoever it is necessary; and know that wheresoever thou shalt sprinkle this water, it will chase away all phantoms, and they shall be unable to hinder or annoy any.

### Extracts

Liquid extracts: The volume of fluid equals the quantity of dried plant used.

Soft extracts: Are evaporated fluid extracts of ointment-like consistency.

Dry extracts: Have been completely evaporated, and the residue dried and powdered.

### Infusion

Bruise plant and add a quart of water. As tea.

### Tincture

For outside application: 2 oz powdered herbs adding a quart of alcohol. Let stand for 2 weeks.

### Essences

Used like Tinctures. Dissolve 1 or 2 oz essential oil(s) in quart of alcohol.

### Dye

Herb is chopped, ground and placed in cold water overnight. The next day bring the mixture to heat, extracting dye. Strain the herb from the liquid after sufficient extraction, and using the dye-water again bring to heat.

The *Rodale Herb Book* gives an adequate account, including the chemicals used to affect the colours.

# CHAPTER SEVEN
# HERBAL ALCHEMY

**Introduction**

Alchemy and chemistry work quite separately from each other. The chemist works with an infinite number of small variables, but each variable is able to be measured, weighed and analysed, making the chemist the master of his data. Every variable is part of known universal experience although there is always an unknown number of variables. The *quantity* and texture of substance is worked by the chemist making every operation complete, begun and finished at any given time decided by the chemist. The alchemist's role converges with the chemist's role, but, with the alchemist, forces beyond control are at work. No one variable can be considered smaller than any other, measurement is on *quality* not *quantity*, and success or failure cannot be foreseen. The variables involved include the phenomena of cosmic forces: the stars and planets, and the earth itself with its natural forces and elements, all of which combine with the alchemist, who is the mirror by which all react. This in itself gives the necessity for the alchemist to be prepared, so that the operation is carried out under the best physical, moral, psychological and spiritual conditions (of a deep religious, meditative, indifferent state of mind). The power of thought can change the reaction of the forces, or even stop them; the physical body may not have the strength for the tasks demanded. The capture of the forces demands the necessity of ritual, the use of symbology, sound, colour and astrological timing. With the influence of the solar system and the intricate timing of events according to planetary aspects and positions, it is probable that no one experiment can be duplicated in a person's individual lifetime.

The variety of alchemical uses to which herbs can be put is infinite; the previous chapter gives some examples. From the above definition one can see that the products described in the previous chapter, according to alchemy are not complete. Only the recipe and mechanical means of producing one's product is supplied. In addition, the process of the product combined with the 'forces' is not enough. Alchemy starts from the inception of the idea, careful planning of which herb to use and what product to make from it; the meticulous timing (astrological or otherwise) of when the herb is to be picked, dried and prepared; then the process of the product with the care and work involved to operate at the most favourable astrological times, creating the attraction of the required forces; not forgetting preparation of the self (individual) to perform the operation. The working of alchemy can take anything from one hour/one day, to a lifetime.

What will be dealt with in this chapter is the extraction of the essential properties of a herb by distillation. Actual extraction with the use of laboratory equipment *is* 'chemistry'; it is the added variables that make it 'alchemy', which will be explained in the following chapter.

Three basic substances which are dealt with by the alchemist—and without which nothing could be accomplished—are:

Salt          $\ominus$
Sulphur       $\leftfooty$
Mercury       $\mercury$

The Mercury symbol is the same symbol for the planet Mercury, but we are not talking about the same thing. These are the substances found in the three kingdoms of vegetable, animal and mineral; but they are not the same in each kingdom, for they each work on a different vibratory level.

90

Our main concern here is the vegetable kingdom, so our discussion will evolve around this particular kingdom.

From your extraction the oily substance is a combination of Mercury and Sulphur, the ashes from the remaining herb (which is calcined) is the Salt. The Sulphur can be separated from the Mercury by further distillation, but in herbal alchemy this further separation is not as essential as in mineral alchemy. In the forming of the alchemical spagyric medicine or elixir, the oil extract and the final product of the ashes are joined. But for other uses, i.e. oils and incense, the combinations vary along with any points of conjunction necessary in the recipe. All in all, the end result is the same—where Sulphur, Salt and Mercury make up the final product.

The following notes should clarify the above comments.

### Extraction

Frater Albertus in the *Alchemist's Handbook* provides a simple explanation on distillation. He also points out that dried herbs are best used in this method, for the water from the fresh herbs would cause extra bulk which would have to be distilled off; also, the dried herb still contains the three substances—Sulphur, Salt and Mercury. However, there are some alchemists who believe short-cuts must not be made and only the fresh, whole plant be used, as in the drying, vital properties are lost.

### *Menstrum*

Rectified alcohol for use in the apparatus should be of sufficient amount, and the following explains this preparation of the menstrum. But first I will stress that if the final product is to be taken internally, then non-drinkable or poisonous alcohol must not be used. Other menstrums are: water, distilled water, dew, oil and ether. If using ether extra care must be taken due to its high volatility: do not have any exposed flame or pilot light nearby, and work quickly avoiding long exposure to the air. Handle ether out of doors, as the fumes can cause a severe reaction if inhaled in sufficient quantity.

Alcohol, or spirit of wine, obtained from wine is the best basis for one's menstrum as it is claimed to be of the highest vibratory rate of any essence in the vegetable kingdom, and the closest to man's vibrations.

***To rectify wine:*** First obtain a red, mature, unfortified wine, as close to 15-16% proof alcohol as possible, 17% or more in any wine will probably give an unpure end result as the additives would no doubt have been added to the wine. Distil at no higher than 78°C, which is boiling point for alcohol, any higher will bring over too much water. At altitudes higher than sea level the temperature will be lower. Once about 3 teaspoons have come over into your receiving vessel, test the first distillate by pouring some in a teaspoon, light a match and pass the flame across the teaspoon to see if the liquid lights up. This flame is invisible, therefore hold your hand at least six inches above the teaspoon to test for the heat from the flame. If no flame, then phlegm has come over (which is natural for the first distillate); this is poisonous and must be thrown out. Continue your distillation and test as before. Continue until you get a flame, then you can retain the distillate assuming that alcohol is now coming over. Decant regularly into a clean airtight jar. When your percentage of alcohol has come over (this is decided by the quantity of wine left in your retort or distilling flask) recommence your testing. When no flame occurs you know the process is at an end and you will get no more alcohol from your wine.

The teaspoon testing method is also a way of telling the quantity of water in your distilled alcohol. Take the residue wine and throw it away, wash your distilling flask and pour your decanted first distillate into your flask and repeat distillation but at a lower temperature. This should take place at least seven times overall if you want a very pure, proof ethyl alcohol.

To get a very subtle Spirit of Wine at the first distilling, take some bread straight from the oven while still hot, break it in half and hang the bread in a jar containing wine, but not touching the wine. Seal the jar and leave the bread there long enough to be swollen with the 'spirit' of the wine. Repeat this with more bread if more is needed, then place the bread in your distilling apparatus and distil over the Spirit of Wine, which can be rectified through circulation. Note that the bread must be placed into glass apparatus.

**Liebig Condenser** With the Liebig condenser the menstrum and the herbs are boiled together in a flask to which the condenser is attached. This distilling flask has a side arm which attaches to a long glass tube (condenser) which is surrounded by an outer jacket. Cold water passes continuously through this jacket from a tap, through the bottom opening and drains out through the top opening, through a tube and into a drain. The vapour from the flask goes out through the inner tube of the condenser, where it cools and condenses, then as a liquid runs from the condenser into the collecting vessel. A thermometer is placed through the cork at the top of the flask to gauge the boiling temperature. The bulb of the thermometer must not be placed in the liquid—it sits in the vapour. The flask should not be more than half full to allow for expansion, and the collecting vessel must not be sealed to the condenser, for if it is there would be an explosion, and if it is sealed there must also be an airpressure tap attached which is left slightly on for a constant release of pressure. The contents of the flask must not be heated until dry, for the flask may crack.

**Retort** This is an all-glass vessel which has a long stem with a wide opening at the vessel end, tapering to a small opening at the stem end. A small opening is also at the top of the bulb with a glass stopper, or an adapter, and thermometer. The end of the neck is attached to a double-neck receiving flask, which has in its second neck an adjustable pressure tap. The Retort is used for distillation. This method also boils the herb in the menstrum, and the stem performs the same function as the condenser. In this case there is no automatic cooling, so one must be in constant supervision cooling the stem with a cloth which is soaked in cold water. The use of a water bath would also be advisable to prevent the Retort from over-heating and cracking. It is also necessary to have some sort of holder as the Retort could get rather hot.

   ***Soxhlet Distillation*** The selected herb must be finely ground in a mortar with a pestle, then placed in the thimble of the extraction apparatus. This apparatus is attached to a flask which is half filled with the rectified alcohol as explained above. A bunsen burner or some sort of fire is lighted under the flask when commencing the extraction.

   There are 3 parts to the Soxhlet extraction apparatus: the flask, which holds the menstrum; the extractor and thimble, of which the thimble (a filter paper cylinder) holds the herb; and the condenser, which is connected to running water by tubing. The flask is attached at the bottom of the extractor, which is the middle section. The thimble is in the extractor. The condenser rests on the extractor as the top section. This is illustrated at the end of this chapter.

   Frater Albertus stated that after three or four extractions a definite change of colour is noticed in the contents of the flask. From this statement we are assuming that Frater Albertus replaces the contents of the thimble every few hours with fresh herbs; this process taking a total of about 48 hours. The herb replaced (dead matter or faeces) is kept in a porcelain or earthenware dish for later calcining.

   The flame from the burner must be moderate, otherwise the sulphur (extract) will be scorched and lose its efficacy. This is shown by a dark rim in the distilling flask (bulb).

   A water bath rather than an open flame is preferable, as the water bath prevents severity of scorching or burning of the soil (Sulphur) contained in the extract (essence—Mercury).

The alcohol travelling through the syphon tube eventually turns clear, which indicates that the extraction is completed for each thimble of herbs. The thimble is then removed and the contents placed in the prepared earthenware or porcelain dish. A wire screen is placed over the dish and the residue is lighted, which should ignite at once because of saturation from the alcohol. There must be no other flammable substances near by. The burning substance should be calcined to a black ash. This ash is ground in a mortar and then returned to the dish, where it is calcined again to a light grey ash. Prolonged calcination changes the light grey/white ash to a reddish colour, which is preferable, but would take a greater amount of time. The light grey ashes are sufficient.

At this stage the alcohol (to be saved for future use) can be distilled off by the use of the Retort or the Liebig Condenser (as explained earlier), though some do not perform this separation. It would depend on the desired end product. At this point I will give two operations which can be followed which I will call (a) and (b).

(*a*)    Place the calcined ashes (Salt) into the lower flask (the extract has already been removed to another container). The oily extract is poured over the Salt just enough to cover it. The flask is re-attached to the apparatus and the circulation is continued until there is no change in colour and the salt has absorbed all that is possible. The clear extract is poured out of the flask (saved) and more essence is added to the Salt, until the Salt does not absorb any more.

At the end of this process you will have the Alchemical Elixir at its 'first stage'; an oily substance when warm and a solid substance when cold. This process can be continued by recalcining and a repetition of the circulation process. Each time the potency is increased. A further step is by placing the Sulphur, Salt and Mercury combined into a glass jar and sealing it, leaving it in a moderate heat for digestion. A stone in the vegetable kingdom is formed but this is not a philosopher's stone. This stone is extremely potent compared to any form of elixir. This herbal stone attracts the Mercury, Sulphur and Salt or other herbs when merely immersed (i.e. immersed in water that contains a herb. The Sulphur and Mercury separate from the herb and float to the top of the water. One can then distil these off then calcine the herb for the salt.).

(*b*)     This method uses half alcohol and half distilled water. When distilling off the alcohol keep the first part that was distilled and place it in a small dropper-bottle and seal. When most of the alcohol has been distilled off place it in a seal-tight bottle to use on another batch of herbs. Do not dry the essence in the flask, for the flask is liable to crack. (What moisture is left is water, for alcohol distils before water.) You must take the remaining substance, evaporate it, and calcine it in a dish, as was explained earlier. It should be calcined to white-grey; this will happen quite quickly. Put the white Sulphur and the soluble salts into the dropper-bottle with the earlier separated extracted alcohol. The reason for taking the first part of the extracted alcohol is that this part usually holds the scent of the herb. Let this digest in a gentle heat (sandbath) 40°C for 1-2 weeks, then distil over again. The distillate is your tincture.

It is suggested by Albertus here that this herbal tincture (if taken as a medicine) is taken in a little wine, fruit juice, or water each morning for one year. About seven drops is more than enough in one glass.[1]

---

[1] From a homeopathic view this is not advisable unless the spagyric tincture is one that will treat a specific weakness or ailment. When choosing a herb for this work, be sure that you choose the right one. A homeopath should be able to help you there through diagnosis of your physical, mental and emotional health.

## Maceration, Enfleurage and Extraction

The following three methods of Maceration, Enfleurage and Extraction are used when dealing with a herb whose oils would normally be destroyed or lost through distillation.

### Maceration

Maceration is generally used with flowers which deteriorate immediately after picking.

1    The ground herb is placed in a flask, bottle or container.

2    Menstrum is poured over the herb to produce the extract (strong alcohol, preferably brandy). In a previous chapter it was shown how oil was used as a menstrum, but this *cannot* be taken internally.

3    Seal tight the container and place near a furnace in the winter (or warmth provided by some other method). Heat should not exceed that required to hatch an egg.

4    Half or one third of container should be left empty, leaving room for expansion and pressure build-up.

5    After several days/weeks the menstrum colour will have changed.

6    When sufficiently macerated, the liquid is sieved into a clean glass container.

7    The remaining herb is calcined.

8    Place still warm ashes into a preheated flask, add extracted liquid (macerated herb) and seal flask to prevent alcohol fumes from escaping.

9    Place in moderately heated conditions for digestion for about 2 weeks. The salt should absorb the essence.

At this stage it is ready to be used as medication or otherwise. This product is harmless but of high potency, and should be taken internally in very small, *diluted* amounts.

Another process of maceration is to immerse the freshly picked flowers into hot fat. In this method the fat penetrates the flowers' cell walls and dissolves the flower oil present. Many batches are repeated in the same hot fat until the perfume saturates the fat. Then the fat is cooled, and this stage is called the 'pomade' and can be used.

To get an extraction from a 'pomade' one washes the fat with high proof alcohol which dissolves the flower oil. The end result, though, has a 'fatty by-note'. This can be taken a step further by distilling off the alcohol.

### Enfleurage

Enfleurage is used with flowers that continue their physiological functions for a time after picking. This is generally used on large-scale production where rectangular wooden chassis, each holding a glass plate on each side, are put together (one on top of the other) to form air-tight compartments. The glass plates are each smeared with a pure fat, strewn with flowers, then placed together. This process is repeated daily for as long as one wishes, depending on the perfume strength needed; for example, Jasmine takes 70 days. Extraction from the Pomade is as for maceration.

### Extraction

The fresh flowers, and/or herb material, are placed inside extractors where contact is made with a volatile solvent, and essential oil, waxes, colours, etc., are extracted. Distillation removes the solvent, leaving a semi-solid end product.

### Water and Steam Distillation

With the distillation train, the Lieburg Condenser, or a Retort, the herb is boiled in water. With the Soxhlet, the water steam passes through the herb. The resulting volatile vapours pass into a condenser, where they are cooled and so are converted back into liquid form. They are then passed into an oil separator where the oil and water form two distinct layers. Both layers can be drained off separately, giving you the natural essential oil.

With this method the plant is used fresh. It is cut up and the seeds broken, etc., to expose as many oil glands as possible. Distillation must take place immediately after the plant has been picked and cut up, as the oil evaporates quite fast from the fresh plant once cut.

### Water distillation
For water distillation the plant is immersed in water. In some cases this is important, for some plants (e.g. Rose petals) become a glutinous mass when exposed to steam, whereas in water the oil distilled is increased.

### Water and steam distillation
This is when a grid is inserted above the water level and the herb sits on top of the grid. The steam and not the water facilitates the diffusion of oil. This method is the most commonly used.

### Steam distillation
There is a steam distillation method which is technically advanced to the two above methods. The steam passes through the plant and so facilitates diffusion. This, however, leads to problems if the moisture in the plant material evaporates before the oil is fully released.

Some essential oil constituents are partly water soluble and are not always separated in the oil separation. When this occurs, the separated water must be brought to the boil again (cohabitation). Rose oil and orange flower oil are treated this way to recover the dissolved oil.

The inadequacy of water and steam distillation is that some of the delicate constituents of the oil may be affected, and some of the constituents which dissolve partially in the distillation water cannot be readily recovered. In addition, the oil may not be volatile in steam.

*Notes*
Water and steam distillation is normally used on fresh herbs, and the use of alcohol as a menstrum is used on dried herbs.

This is because the alcohol will damage the fresh herb as it dissolves the water and chlorophyll of the plant, producing in some cases a disagreeable odour, or a dark solid mass.

Where possible, use collected dew as the substance in all your experiments. The herbs are washed in dew, and dew can be used for the distilled water for the menstrum. Dew has the etheric life essence, and with its use the magical potency of anything you make will be increased. Armand Barbault in *Gold of a Thousand Mornings* explains how he made the Elixir of Life by using dew.

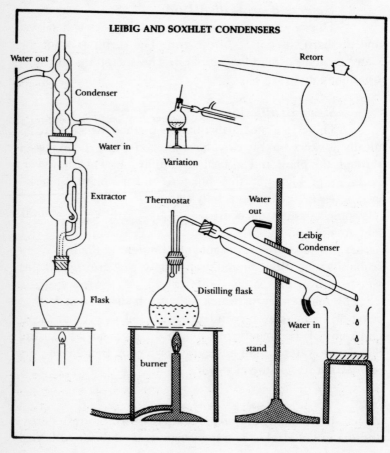

**LEIBIG AND SOXHLET CONDENSERS**

# CHAPTER EIGHT
# RITUAL

The impregnation of vital forces, higher powers and the cosmic energies into an object or a desired happening is an essential part of magic, from the making of an amulet to the obtaining of the higher genius. To this end, I include this chapter.

There are many symbols of Alchemy and almost all have different meanings. One in particular which is useful is Dee's Hieroglyphic Monad. Some ascribe this symbol to the elusive spirit Mercurius—the Alpha Et Omega of Alchemy. Depending on the system one uses there are many steps in Alchemy; most are related back to the planets and zodiac. The Monad, for example, is representative of the seven major planets (of old) which relate to the seven stage system.

Symbol of Dee's                    Planetary
Hieroglyphic Monad                 Breakdown

$$= \begin{array}{ll} \hbar \text{ Saturn} & \text{♁ ♓ ♂ Mars} \\ \text{♐ ♃ Jupiter} & \text{♀ Venus} \\ \text{♆ ♀ Mercury} & \text{☉ Sun ♌ Moon} \end{array}$$

When dealing with magical associations it must be remembered that all symbols emit power. The talismatic aspect of the hermetic work with herbs is very evident in this respect. If a symbol of Dee's Monad, for example, is placed in the laboratory of the Alchemist, and the Alchemist meditates on the planetary aspect of the symbol with which he is about to work, he can form an emphatic link to that planet. The

Monad itself is a complex form of symbology covering a wide range of scientific applications, but for the purposes of this book it will suffice to relate it to the planets and their alchemic associations.

A ritualistic method has been given, as used in 'The Magical Society of the Golden Dawn'. A basis of this procedure is adequately outlined in *The Golden Dawn* by I. Regardie, but the system is not for beginners. For those of a serious mind towards alchemy it will show how a modern system of magic can be utilised. The Golden Dawn Society was founded in England in 1888 and put together most of the profound occult teachings into a workable system of magic. The Order changed its name in 1900 as the result of a fragmentation within the ranks, but the system and its rituals carried on in both the UK, USA, and in New Zealand where it has undergone a revival and major overhaul under the name of 'Smaragdum Thalasses'. The basic outline is taken from an Order paper called Z2, which gives the process to use during an alchemical working. The very powerful invocations referred to but not given in this text are part of the Order's Enochian system of magic, but I do advise people who wish to utilise the methods supplied, to place names of power they themselves are familiar with. To a great many the Z2 formula may be long-winded and meaningless, but to the initiated it will show a synthesis of Order teaching in creating the herbal elixir. The whole process involved requires the power of the forces to be injected into the elixir at the correct moment, so that over a period of time the astral potency of the elixir can increase.

Below is the Z2 formula with some added notes in brackets, followed by a few comments.

## Z2 Formula

*Alchemy*

**A**    The Curcurbite or the Alembic (the flask including the apparatus).

**B**    The Alchemist.

**C**    The processes and forces employed. (Have with you a record of what you must do along with the list of planetary forces to be used and the names of power, the prepared ritual, etc.)

**D**    The Matter to be transmuted. (Herb and Menstrum.)

**E**    The selection of the Matter to be transmuted, and the formation (method), cleansing and disposing of all the necessary vessels, materials, etc., for the working of the process. (In other words 'be prepared'.)

**F**    Purifications, and banishings of work area (temple). General Invocation of the Higher Forces to Action. Place Matter within the curcurbite or philosophic egg (within the place it must go depending on the apparatus in use, and the placing of the Menstrum in its respective place for the operation), and invocation of a blind force to action therein in darkness and silence. (The blind force is the zodiac and planetary force of the herb by use of Pentagrams and Hexagrams.)

**G**    The beginning of the actual process. The regulation and restriction of the proper degree of heat and moisture to be employed in the working. First evocation followed by the first distillation. (Evocation given to nature of working.)

**H**    The taking up of the residuum which remaineth after the distillation from the curcurbite or alembic; the grinding thereof to form a powder in a mortar. (The calcining takes place first.) This powder (Salt) is then to be placed again in the curcurbite. The fluid already distilled is to be poured again on it. The curcurbite or philosophic egg is to be closed.

**I**    The curcurbite or philosophic egg being hermetically sealed, the Alchemist announces aloud that all is prepared for the invocation of the forces necessary to accomplish the work. The Matter is then to be placed upon an Altar with the elements and four weapons thereon (earth—salt; air—incense; water—cup with consecrated water; fire—red candle. Your elemental weapons—cup; dagger; pentacle; wand), upon the white triangle and upon a flashing talisman of a general nature, in harmony with the matter selected for the working. Standing now in the place of the Hierophant at the East of the Altar (the temple is set up as for the 0°=0° grade in the G.D. outer Order), the Alchemist should place his left hand upon the top of the curcurbite (flask), raise his right hand holding the Lotus wand by the Aries band (in Southern Hemisphere the Libra band representing the beginning of the year), ready to commence the general invocation of the forces of the Divine Light to operate in the work.

**J** The pronouncing aloud of the Invocation of the requisite general forces, answering to the class of alchemical work to be performed. The conjuring of the necessary forces to act in the curcurbite for the work required. The tracing in the air above it with appropriate weapon the necessary lineal figures, signs, sigils and the like. Then let the Alchemist say: 'So help me the Lord of the Universe and my own Higher Soul'. Then let him raise the curcurbite in the air with both hands, saying: 'Arise herein to action, O ye forces of the Light Divine'.

**K** Now let the matter putrefy in the water bath in a very gentle heat, until darkness beginneth to supervene; and even until it becometh entirely black. (This refers to the digestion and deepening of colour, not necessarily black.) If from its nature the mixture will not admit entire blackness, examine it astrally until there is the astral appearance of the thickest possible darkness, and thou mayest also evoke an elemental form to tell thee if the blackness be sufficient. But be thou sure that in this latter thou art not deceived, seeing that the nature of such an elemental will be deceptive from the nature of the symbol of darkness, wherefore ask thou of him nothing further concerning the working at this stage but only concerning the blackness, and this can be further tested by the elemental itself, which should be either black or clad in an intensely black robe. (Note, that for the evocation use the names, etc., of Saturn.) When the mixture be sufficiently black, then take the curcurbite out of the water bath and place it north of the Altar and perform over it a solemn invocation of the forces of Saturn to act therein; holding the wand (Lotus wand) by the black band, then say: 'The voice of the Alchemist said unto me, let me enter the Path of Darkness, for thus may I achieve the realm of Light'. The curcurbite is then to be unstopped and the Alembic Head fitted on for purposes of distillation. (This is the reconnection of the apparatus for distilling. Note also that during the invocations an unconsecrated flashing talisman is placed under the curcurbite to attract the necessary forces. This is done by colour, the colour attracting a particular vibration.)

**L**    Then let the Alchemist distil with a gentle heat until nothing remaineth to come over. Let him take the residuum (calcine it) and grind it into a powder; replace this powder in the curcurbite, and pour again upon it the fluid previously distilled. The curcurbite is then to be placed again in a water bath in a gentle heat. When it seems fairly dissolved (irrespective of colour) let it be taken out of the bath. It is now to undergo another magical ceremony.

**M**    Now place the curcurbite to the West of the Altar, holding the Lotus wand by the black end, perform a magical invocation of the Moon in her decrease and of Cauda Draconis. The curcurbite is then to be exposed to the moonlight (she being in her decrease) for nine consecutive nights, commencing at full moon. The Alembic Head is then to be fitted on. (The flask is reattached to the rest of the apparatus.)

**N**    Repeat process set forth in Section L.

**O**    The curcurbite is to be placed to the East of the Altar, and the Alchemist performs an invocation of the Moon in her increase, and of Caput Draconis (holding Lotus wand by white band) to act upon the Matter. The curcurbite is now exposed for nine consecutive nights (ending with the full moon) to the Moon's rays. (In this, as in all similar exposures, it matters not if such nights are over-clouded, so long as the vessel be placed in such a position as to receive the direct rays should the clouds clear.)

**P** The curcurbite is again to be placed on the white triangle upon the Altar. The Alchemist performs an invocation of the forces of the Sun to act in the curcurbite. It is then to be exposed to the rays of the Sun for 12 hours each day from 8.30 a.m. to 8.30 p.m. (or Sunrise to Sunset, and the Sun must be strongly aspected and positioned in the Zodiac at this stage).

**Q** The curcurbite is again placed upon the white triangle upon the Altar. The Alchemist repeats the words: 'Child of Earth, Long has thou dwelt in darkness, quit the night and seek the day,' then holding the Lotus wand by the white end, say: 'I formulate in thee the invoked forces of Light', then reciting the mystic words (words of Power from the Enochian Watch Towers).

At this point keen and bright flashes of light should appear in the curcurbite, and the mixture itself (as far as nature will permit) should be clear. Now invoke an Elemental from the curcurbite consonant to the Nature of the mixture, and judge by the nature of the colour of its robes and their brilliancy whether the Matter has attained the right condition. But if the flashes do not appear and if the robes of the elemental be not brilliant and flashing, then let the curcurbite stand within the white triangle for 7 days; having on the right hand of the Apex of the triangle a flashing (gold) talisman of the Sun, and in the left one of the Moon (silver). Let it not be moved or disturbed all these 7 days; but not in the dark, save at night. Then let the operation as aforementioned be repeated over the curcurbite and this process may be repeated altogether three times if the flashing light cometh not. For without this latter the work would be useless. But if after three repetitions it still appear not, it is a sign that there hath been an error in the working, such being either in the disposition of the Alchemist or in the management of the curcurbite. Wherefore let the lunar and solar invocations and exposures be repeated, when without doubt, if these be done with care (and more especially those of Caput Draconis and Cauda Draconis with those of the moon as taught, for these have great force materially), then without doubt shall that flashing light manifest itself in the curcurbite.

**R**     Holding the Lotus wand by the white end, the Alchemist now draws over the curcurbite the symbol of the Flaming Sword as if descending into the mixture. Then let him place the curcurbite to the East of the Altar. The Alchemist stands between the pillars, and performs a solemn invocation of the forces of Mars to act therein. The curcurbite is then placed between the pillars (or drawn symbols of the same) for seven days, upon the flashing talisman of Mars. After this period, fit on the Alembic Head, and distil first in a water bath then direct flame until what time the mixture be all distilled over.

**S**     Now let the Alchemist take the fluid of the distillate and let him perform over it an invocation of the forces of Mercury (planet) to act in the clear fluid, so as to formulate therein the alchemical Mercury, even the Mercury of the philosophers. (The residuum or the dead head is not to be worked with at present, but is to be set apart for future use.) After the invocation of the Alchemic Mercury a certain brilliance should manifest itself in the whole fluid, that is to say, it should not only be clear, but also brilliant and flashing. Now expose it in an hermetic receiver for seven days to the light of the Sun (and when Mercury is in strong harmonious aspects); at the end of which time there should be distinct flashes of light therein. (Or a philosophic egg may be used; but the receiver of the Alembic if close-stopped will answer this purpose.)

**T**     Now the residuum or Dead Head is to be taken out of the curcurbite (calcined), ground small and replaced. An invocation of the Forces of Jupiter is then to be performed over that Powder. It is then to be kept in the dark, standing upon a flashing Talisman of Jupiter for seven days. At the end of this time there should be a slight flashing about it, but if this come not yet, repeat this operation up to three times, when a faint flashing of light is certain to come.

**U**     A flashing Talisman (tablet) of each of the four elements is now to be placed upon an altar as shown in the diagram below, and thereon are also to be placed the magical elemental weapons, as is also clearly indicated. The receiver containing the distillate is now to be placed between the Air and Water Talismans (tablets), and the curcurbite with the Dead Head between the Fire and Earth Talismans (tablets). Now let the Alchemist perform an invocation using especially the Supreme Ritual of the Pentagram, and the lesser magical implement appropriate. First, of the forces of Fire to act in the curcurbite on the Dead Head. Second, of those of Water to act on the distillate. Third, of the forces of the Spirit to act on both (using white end of the Lotus wand). Fourth, of those of the

Air to act on the distillate; and lastly, those of the Earth to act on the Dead Head. Let the curcurbite and the receiver stand thus for five consecutive days, at the end of which time there should be flashes manifest in both mixtures. And these flashes should be lightly coloured.

**V**    The Alchemist, still keeping the vessels in the same relative positions, but removing the tablets of the elements from the Altar, then substitutes one of Kether. This must be White with golden charges, and is to be placed within the white triangle between the vessels. He then addresses a most solemn invocation to the forces of Kether; to render the result of the working that which he shall desire, and making over each vessel the symbol of the flaming sword.

This is the most important of all the invocations. It will only succeed if the Alchemist keepeth himself closely allied unto his Higher Self, ensuring the working of the invocation and of making the Talisman. And at the end of it, if it have been successful, a keen and translucent flash will take place of the slightly coloured flashes in the receiver of the curcurbite; so that the fluid should sparkle as a diamond, whilst the powder in the curcurbite shall slightly gleam.

**W**    The distilled liquid is now to be poured from the receiver upon the residuum of the Dead Head in the curcurbite, and the mixture at first will appear cloudy. It is now to be exposed to the Sun for ten days consecutively (ten is Tiphareth translating the influence of Kether). It is then again to be placed upon the white triangle upon the Altar, upon a flashing talisman of Venus, with a solemn invocation of Venus to act therein. Let it remain thus for seven days, at the end of which time see what forms and colour and appearance the liquor hath taken, for there should now arise a certain softer flash in the liquid, and an elemental may be evoked to test the condition. When this softer flash is manifest, place the curcurbite into the water bath to digest with a very gentle heat for seven days. Place it then in a water bath for distilling, beginning with a gentle, and ending with a strong heat. Distil thus until nothing more will come over, even with a most violent heat. (Not recommended as the equipment may break.) Preserve the fluid in a closely stoppered vial, it is an Elixir for use according to the substance from which it was prepared. If from a thing medicinal, a medicine; if from a metal, for the purifying of metals; and herein shalt thou use thy judgement. The residuum thou shalt place without powdering into a crucible, well sealed and luted. And thou shalt place the same in thine Athanor, bringing it first to a red, and then to a white head, and thus thou shalt do 7 times in 7 consecutive days, taking out the crucible each day as soon as thou hast brought it to the highest possible heat, and allowing it to cool gradually.

And the preferable time for this working should be in the heat of the day. On the seventh day of this operation thou shalt open the crucible and thou shalt behold what Form and Colour thy Caput Mortuum hath taken. It will be like either a precious stone or glittering powder. And this stone or powder shall be of Magical Virtue in accordance with its nature.

Naturally, the above will not fit into the method you may use, but the purpose of the Z2 was to give the student a guideline, a basis, and a formula by which to work. From the Z2 you will know that invocation takes place, that there is a temple setting, flashing talismans used, and that at certain points of the operation one performs the necessary ritual. One can also see that if working with planetary forces, the operation may take months, depending on the planetary movements and aspects formed.

Now I am assuming that the reader has magical knowledge, or ready reference to the same. Due to this assumption I will not be explaining the implements and procedures of practical magic. For those who do not have ready reference, a local occult book supplier could assist. I would suggest books such as *The Golden Dawn* and *How to make and use Talismans* by I. Regardie, *Liber E & Liber O* by A. Crowley, and *The Secret*

*Temple* by Robert Wang. In all cases it must be remembered that the Alchemists normally write their own ceremonies according to the nature of their workings, therefore all I really can supply is a guideline by the later, and the following formats.

### Talismans

When a flashing Talisman is referred to in the Z2, it is generally a flat object of virgin paper, coloured the colour of the planetary force to be called on, and with drawings of sigils and seals of said planet, in the complementary colour. One can use disks of metal of the nature of the planet but this is rather expensive.

When using the planetary squares and seals of the alchemical work with the operation, the talisman used is not a charged or consecrated one, as this forms a completely different function and directs its rays to (for example) directly healing an individual from a trapped force within the Kamea. But in the above type of alchemical working the Kamea is in fact a force magnet. It attracts the planetary force by virtue of its colour and shape, and links to the energy within the flask, strengthening the content's properties. Though the vital essence is within the flask, the energy field of this essence extends beyond the glass. A dark-coloured glass restricts this energy of the essence and acts as a filter to external contaminations.

### Kameas and Seals

For the use of Kameas and Seals I would suggest one uses the planetary seal and sigil of the archangel of the planet as a force sufficient to help with the operation. The Sigils of the other aspects of planetary forces should be left alone, unless one is familiar with their functions.

### Alternative method

Another form of ceremonial work is where chosen

assorted herbs are collected then placed in some oil (olive oil) in a mortar. These herbs are ground up in the oil. During the whole operation the mind of the Alchemist must be concentrating on the purpose for which the oil is to be made.

The Spirit of Actives and the Spirit of Passives are invoked (pentagrams) and a few chosen words stating the operation and purpose, calling on the blessing of Adoni and the angelic beings, giving names concerned with the nature of the herbs, which in turn affect the nature of the operation. The planetary force is invoked by use of hexagrams with a coloured talisman placed under the mixture (as explained previously). The mixture would have been put into a glass jar which is left to digest in a warm place with daily invocations for 7 days. (Each day of the week is a different planetary day, hence the planetary force of the day is invoked, along with the pentagrams of passive or active, depending on the nature of the planet, along with the element pentagrams.) The mixture is then strained, and the faeces calcined then blended with the liquid.

The final product is hermetically sealed in a consecrated container. This final product should emit an energy and flashing lights.

One could use any form of experiment with this method, the beauty of which is that there need not be a temple set up or special magical weapons. It can take place in any place, the tools being the operator's hands, voice and will. All one has to do is, before each working, to clear the area with the banishing pentagram ritual. Note never to banish over the elixir but to banish around it.

The amount of days for digestion depends on the operator and the product required. One could extend the process over any length of time, working in with the moon cycle and/or planetary movements. Consider the previous discussion on careful timing of operations, astrologically and otherwise, for this is very important.

# APPENDIX 1
# ELEMENTS AND SYMBOLS

## Elements

△: FIRE
△ of △:     Fiery part of fire
▽ of △:     Watery part of fire
△ of △:     Airy part of fire
▽ of △:     Earthy part of fire

▽: WATER
△ of ▽:     Fiery part of water
▽ of ▽:     Watery part of water
△ of ▽:     Airy part of water
▽ of ▽:     Earthy part of water

△: AIR
△ of △:     Fiery part of air
▽ of △:     Watery part of air
△ of △:     Airy part of air
▽ of △:     Earthy part of air

▽: EARTH
△ of ▽:     Fiery part of earth
▽ of ▽:     Watery part of earth
△ of ▽:     Airy part of earth
▽ of ▽:     Earthy part of earth

## Zodiac

| | |
|---|---|
| ♈: | Aries |
| ♉: | Taurus |
| ♊: | Gemini |
| ♋: | Cancer |
| ♌: | Leo |
| ♍: | Virgo |
| ♎: | Libra |
| ♏: | Scorpio |
| ♐: | Sagittarius |
| ♑: | Capricorn |
| ♒: | Aquarius |
| ♓: | Pisces |

## Planets

| | |
|---|---|
| ☉: | Sun |
| ☽: | Moon |
| ☿: | Mercury |
| ♀: | Venus |
| ♂: | Mars |
| ♃: | Jupiter |
| ♄: | Saturn |
| ♅: | Uranus |
| ♆: | Neptune |
| ♇: | Pluto |

# APPENDIX 2

A listing of herbs under planets is followed by a listing of herbs under signs.

* represents a herb also listed under another planet or sign.
'*Others*' represents herbs not listed in Chapter 5.

### Herbs under planets

**Sun**
Almond
Aloe*
Angelica
Ash Tree
Bay Laurel*
Bean
Benzoin
Borage*
Buttercup
Camomile
Camphor
Carline Thistle
Cassia
Cinnamon
Cloves*
Corn*
Daffodil
Dandelion*
Eucalyptus
Frankincense
Galbanum*
Ginseng

Goto Cola
Heliotrope
High Joan the Conqueress
Juniper*
Lemon
Marigold
Mastic*
Mistletoe
Myrrh
Oak
Olibanum
Olive*
Rosemary*
Rowan
Rue
Saffron
St John's Wort
Storax*
Sunflower
Walnut

*Others*: Calamus, Celandine,
Centaury, Coconut,
Eyebright, Grapefruit,
Helianthus, Honey,
Honewort, Lignum Vitae,
Pimpernel*, Tormentil,
Turnsole.

**Moon**
Anise
Barley
Bay Laurel
Camphor*
Cucumber
Cyclamen*

Fennel*
Forget-me-nots
Galbanum*
Honeysuckle
Hyssop*
Lettuce
Lily of the Valley
Lily (water)
Lily (yellow)
Lotus
Moonwort
Mushroom (Psilocybe)
Nutmeg
Olibanum
Orris Root
Poppy (white)
Pumpkin
Rose (white)
Rose (yellow)
Rosemary
Sandalwood*
Sorrel
Willow
Wintergreen
*Others*: Adder's Tongue,
Arrowhead, Banana, Bayleaf,
Breadfruit, Cabbage,
Caltrops, Cedar, Chickweed,
Dog's Tooth, Endive, Gourd,
Lady's Smock, Mango,
Melon, Mouse-ear, Orphine,
Rattlegrass, Rhubarb,
Seaweed, Sour-Sap,
Stonecrop, Sugarcane,
Trefoil, Turnip, Watercress,
Waterflag.

117

**Mercury**
Acacia*
Bergamot
Calamint
Caraway
Cascarilla Bark
Chicory*
Coltsfoot
Corn
Dill
Dragon's Wort*
Fennel
Fern (male)
Horehound
Jasmine
Lads Love
Lavender
Lime
Linden
Lungwort
Mandrake*
Marjoram*
Mint
Mace
Oregano
Parsley
Parsnip
Pine*
Sandalwood
Savory
Tansy*
Thyme
Valerian
Verbena
Walnut*

*Others*: Amara-dulcis,
Azaleas, Brazil Nut, Carrot,
Cashew, Celery Seed,
Cinnamon Wood,
Elecampane, Fenugreek,
Hazel, Licorice, Maiden Hair
(fern), Myrtle Tree, Oats,
Parsnip, Pomegranate,
Smallage, Southernwood.

### *Venus*
Almond oil*
Amaranth
Apple
Ash*
Bean*
Benzoin*
Birch*
Calamus
Carnation
Catnip
Cinquefoil
Clove
Coltsfoot*
Cowslip*
Cyclamen
Cypress*
Daisy
Dandelion*
Elder*
Fern (female)
Feverfew*
Fig Tree*
Foxglove
Geranium
Groundsel

Ivy
Jasmine*
Ladies Mantle
Lovage
Mandrake*
Meadowsweet
Mint*
Motherwort
Mugwort*
Musk
Nutmeg*
Peppermint
Periwinkle
Pimpernel
Plantain*
Rose
Sandalwood*
Sorrel*
Storax
Strawberry
Tansy*
Teasel
Thyme*
Verbena*
Violet*
*Others*: Alder, Alehoof,
Alkanet, Almond Oil,
Archangle, Arrach,
Artichoke, Bishop's Weed,
Blackberry, Blites, Bramble,
Bugle, Cherry, Chestnut,
Cockshead, Crabsclaws,
Cranes-bill, Crosswort,
Cudweed, Devil's Bit, Drop
Wort, Elderberry, Eryngo,
Foxglove, Lovebush, Peach

Tree, Plums, Pomegranate,
Primrose, Ragwort,
Raspberry, Red Cherry,
Soapwort, Spearmint,
Throatwort, Wheat.

### Mars
Acacia
Aloe
Arnica
Basil
Birds Tongue
Bryony (red)
Camphire
Civet
Coriander
Dragon's Blood
Flaxseed
Garlic
Ginger
Hawthorn
Hemlock*
Hops
Horseradish
Horsetail
Houndstongue
Hyssop*
Iris
Ironwood
Juniper
Lotus (rose)
Milfoil
Milk Thistle
Mustard
Nettle
Onion

Pepper
Pine*
Plantain*
Rose (red)
Witchhazel
Wormwood*
*Others*: Boxtree, Broom,
Cactus, Capers, Crowfoot,
Cypress, Dogwood,
Dovesfoot, Gentian, Ground
Pine, Hedge Hyssop*,
Horsetongue, Madder,
Mouse-tail, Pepperwort,
Sarsaparilla, Savin.

### *Jupiter*
Almond*
Ash*
Balm
Betony
Blue Flag
Borage
Burdock
Cedarwood
Chervil
Chicory
Cinquefoil*
Clove*
Dandelion*
Fig Tree
Hyssop
Jasmine*
Lotus (blue)
Lungwort*
Mint*
Mistletoe*

Myrrh*
Nutmeg*
Oak*
Olive
Rosemary*
Saffron*
Sage*
Tansy*
Thorn Apple*
Violet
*Others*: Alexander, Apricot,
Asparagus, Avens, Bilberry,
Black Currant, Bugloss,
Chestnut, Liverwort*,
Lungwort*, Maple,
Mulberry, Pimento, Rose
Hips, Turnip.

**Saturn**
Agrimony*
Amaranth*
Asafoetida*
Beech
Belladonna*
Birch
Bloodroot
Cinquefoil
Comfrey
Copal
Cypress
Dragon's Wort
Elder
Fern*
Flaxseed*
Goutwort

Hemlock
Hemp (Indian)*
Horsetail
Mandrake*
Monkshood
Mugwort*
Mullein
Mushroom*
Nightshade
Onion*
Parsnip*
Patchouli
Plantain
Poplar*
Rue*
St John's Wort
Solomon's Seal
Tansy
Tobacco
Vervain
Wintergreen*
*Others*: Aconite,
Amaranthus*, Barrenwort,
Beets, Birdsfoot, Coffee,
Elm-tree, Fleawort,
Goutwort, Groundmoss,
Hawkweed, Heartsease,
Knapweed, Knotgrass,
Navelwort, Oakmoss, Pansy,
Parsnip, Quince, Rhubarb
roots, Rupturewort, Rye,
Sassafras, Sciatica-wort,
Shepherd's Purse, Sloes,
Spinach, Tamarind.

**Uranus**
Anise*
Asafoetida
Birthwort
Clover
Corn*
Galbanum
Henbane
Ladies Mantle
Leek
Marjoram
Nightshade (black)
Pennyroyal
Poplar
Sage
*Others*: Oxalis

**Neptune**
Ambergris
Artemisia (Tarragon)
Bay Laurel*
Cannabis
Cocaine
Cowslip
Dandelion
Dock
Ergot
Hemp (Indian)
Jimson Weed
Mandrake
Morning Glory Seed
Mushroom*
Peyote
Poppy (opium)
Scullcap
Thorn Apple
*Others*: Arctotis

**Pluto**
Agrimony*
Aloe*
Ambergris*
Basil*
Belladonna
White Bryony
Red Bryony*
Cypress*
Feverfew
Hellebore
Ironwood
Monkshood*
Mugwort
Mushroom*
Pine
Pipiltzintzintli
Poppy (black)
Wormwood
*Others*: Pitcher Plant

## Herbs under signs

**Aries**
Aloe*
Ambergris
Bay Laurel
Cinnamon
Clove
Clover
Coriander
Cowslip*
Dock*
Dragon's Blood
Feverfew
Garlic

Ginger
Hops
Hemp (Indian)
Horseradish
Horsetail
Juniper
Marjoram*
Mustard (black)
Myrrh
Nettle
Olibanum
Onion*
Pepper
Peyote*
Poppy (opium)
Scullcap
*Others*: Blackberry, Broom,
Fern, Holly, Mustard,
Radish, Rhubarb, Thistle.

## *Taurus*
Amaranth*
Carline Thistle
Cascarilla Bark
Cinquefoil
Coltsfoot
Corn*
Daisy
Dandelion*
Fern (male & female)
Forget-me-nots
Lime
Linden
Lovage
Lungwort*
Mandrake

Milk Thistle
Mushroom (Psilocybe)
Onion
Orris Root
Pimpernel
Sage
Sorrel
Wintergreen
*Others*: Flax, Gourds,
Larkspur, Myrtle, Spinach.

## *Gemini*

Angelica
Asafoetida
Bergamot
Betony
Bryony (red)
Cannabis
Honeysuckle
Lads Love
Leek
Lungwort
Mastic
Meadow Sweet*
Milfoil*
Mint
Mullein
Oregano
Periwinkle
Poppy (white)
Savory
Tansy*
Thyme
Vervain
Walnut*
*Others*: Dog Grass, Madder,
Privet, Woodbine.

## Cancer
Agrimony*
Angelica*
Anise
Balm (lemon)
Betony* (water)
Blue Flag
Camphor
Caraway
Catnip
Chervil
Dill
Houndstongue*
Hyssop
Jasmine
Mandrake*
Mugwort
Olive
Peppermint
Pumpkin
Violet
Wormwood
*Others*: Alder, Cucumber*,
Honeysuckle, Melons,
Rushes, Squashes.

## Leo
Almond
Anise*
Angelica*
Arnica
Bay Laurel*
Borage*
Burdock
Camomile
Camphor

Cyclamen
Daffodil
Dandelion*
Dill*
Fennel*
Frankincense*
Heliotrope
High Joan the Conqueress
Ironwood
Lavender
Lemon
Lettuce
Marigold
Mint*
Morning Glory Seed
Motherwort
Mistletoe
Olive*
Parsley*
Peyote
Rue
Saffron
Sunflower
Walnut
*Others*: Argaric, Bugloss,
Celandine, Eyebright, Peony.

### *Virgo*
Barley
Bean
Bloodroot*
Bryony (white)
Calamint
Calamus
Cascarilla Bark*
Chicory

Corn
Fennel*
Fig Tree
Ginseng
Houndstongue
Mandrake*
Parsnip
Patchouli
Sandalwood
Scullcap
Valerian*
*Others*: Endive, Millet, Oats,
Privet, Wheat, Woodbine.

## Libra
Agrimony
Aloe
Apple
Balm Tree
Carnation
Cucumber
Dandelion
Foxglove
Galbanum
Groundsel
Hellebore
Meadow Sweet
Mustard (white)
Nightshade
Nightshade (black)
Parsley
Rose
Strawberry
Tansy
Teasel
Tobacco

Violet*
Witchhazel*
*Others*: Heartsease, Lemon
Thyme, Pansy, Primrose,
Watercress.

## Scorpio
Acacia
Amaranth
Artemisia (Tarragon)
Basil
Bean*
Birthwort
Cowslip
Goto Cola
Horehound
Ivy
Ladies Mantle
Leek*
Lily (water)
Milfoil
Musk
Pennyroyal
Storax*
Valerian
Wormwood*
*Others*: Blackthorn, Bramble.

## Sagittarius
Agrimony*
Aloe*
Ash
Beech
Betony* (wood)
Birch
Birds Tongue

Cedarwood
Elder
Eucalyptus
Feverfew*
Hawthorn
Nutmeg
Oak
Poplar
Rowan
Sandalwood*
*Others*: Lignum Aloes*,
Mallows.

### Capricorn
Belladonna
Benzoin
Bloodroot
Buttercup
Cassia
Comfrey
Copal
Dock*
Flaxseed
Goutwort
Hemlock
Hemp (Indian)*
Henbane*
Marjoram
Monkshood
Nightshade*
Pine
Plantain
Poppy (black)
Solomon's Seal
Witchhazel

**Aquarius**
Borage
Cypress
Dragon's Wort
Fennel
Frankincense
Galbanum
Henbane
Iris
Jimson Weed
Moonwort
Myrrh*
Peppermint*
St John's Wort
Thorn Apple
*Others*: Euphorbium,
Spikenard.

**Pisces**
Civet
Cocaine
Dock (water)
Ergot
Geranium
Lily of Valley
Yellow Lily
Lotus
Pipiltzintzintli
Storax
Verbena
Willow
*Others*: Fern, Moss, Seaweed.

# APPENDIX 3

Some suitable methods of extracting essential oil from some of the herbs.

| Herb | Method |
|------|--------|
| Almond (bitter) | expression, distillation |
| Angelica root | distillation |
| Anise | distillation |
| Basil | distillation |
| Bay | distillation |
| Caraway | distillation |
| Carnation | extraction |
| Celery seed | distillation |
| Clary Sage | distillation, extraction |
| Coriander | distillation |
| Dillseed | distillation |
| Dillweed | distillation |
| Fennel (bitter) | distillation |
| Fennel (sweet) | distillation |
| Geranium | extraction |
| Jasmine | extraction |
| Lavender | distillation |
| Lovage | distillation |
| Marjoram | distillation |
| Orange blossom | extraction, distillation, enfleurage/maceratio |
| Oregano | distillation |
| Parsley | distillation |
| Pennyroyal | distillation |
| Peppermint | distillation |
| Pineneedle | distillation |
| Rose | extraction, enfleurage/maceration, distillatic |

| | |
|---|---|
| Rosemary | distillation |
| Sage | distillation |
| Spearmint | distillation |
| Tarragon | distillation |
| Thyme | distillation |
| Valerian | distillation |
| Violet leaves | extraction, enfleurage/maceration |

# APPENDIX 4
# ASTRAL CONTACT WITH
# PLANT LIFE

Within the Golden Dawn's Inner Order, which was known as the R.R.et A.C., those at 5=6 level were introduced to a document called 'skrying in the spirit vision'. This paper gave the bare bones for projecting one's consciousness into the astral, and to make contact with the various entities there. When dealing with plant life one must always remember that they too are living entities, and they can considerably help or hinder an adept when they are being utilised for ritual work. Many of the old Grimores have advocated approaching plants only at certain times in relation to the sap in the plant. For a number of years now, there has been increasing scientific experimentation into plant life and the way they communicate with humans. In the later part of the last century a number of adepti of the Golden Dawn started experimenting along the lines of astral contact with plants, in the hope that plants would be able to help them in their alchemical workings.

This method of plant communication was not really invented by the Golden Dawn but streamlined from the pantheist concept of plant life. The alchemist of old would in many ways try to communicate verbally or mentally with the elixir during its course of transmutation. This does not differ from any basic concept to plant communication.

The following experiments and recorded events, taken from a Golden Dawn Manuscript called *The Book of Wylwn*, are examples of plant communication by extending the individual's aura to that of the plant so that a magnetic link exists and a communication of sorts develops. It is very easy when doing these experiments to let the mind wander, but to verify one's contact communication should be done by more than one adept on a single plant, until one is absolutely sure and familiar enough with the actual vibrational pitch of the contact. A good example is for one person to make a contact, record the visionary work and description of the intelligence of the plant, then compare it with another's work on the same plant. These safeguards are generally only necessary in the initial stage of communication, i.e. while still developing your ability.

Working alchemically with a plant is vastly different from working with a metal. Each has it own level of contact, but the plant is possibly the more accessible for the budding alchemist and gives the adept a chance to expand and experiment with his or her sensitivity, which can be carried over into metal work at a later stage. While it is not proposed that all who work with metals should study herbal alchemy, it is very handy if this is done because one has the opportunity to use the alchemical equipment in safety.

To harmonise with one's surroundings and the elements, contact is really essential, and the use of the Golden Dawn formula is a step in that direction. For those of you who have never tried this before it is suggested that you record everything, and try to make contact with the various plants, flowers and shrubs from the area where you live. In this way the auric vibrations will be more easily detectable to you. It is essential that, during the alchemical ritual, you use this link with the plant or the herb to impregnate its vital forces through your own aura.

An example of some of these contacts is given below to give you an idea of the type of reception one can sometimes expect. One interesting thing that has arisen from the research done in this area is that no plant is, strictly speaking, related to one planetary or elemental vibration. One can only catalogue them under the majority of emanations they emit. This is a truly enjoyable experience for those who are sensitive enough to understand the contacts and how to use them.

Please note that the following examples are not exactly as they were written in *The Book of Wylwn* but have been given in abridged format with some personal points excluded.

### Terminology Used:

Formal Contact: A method of contact used along the lines of the contact method given at the end of this Appendix.

Casual Contact; Where initial intent to contact is followed through not by the full formal method, but by the second half of the contact method, i.e. immediate astral linkage and calling forth spirit of herb, etc., without use of the invocations.

Spontaneous Contact: Contact on the spur of the moment, direct conversation. This method leaves the question as to whether the herb made the first auric connection, immediately tuning one into the plant's auric field.

### *Example One*

Casual Contact: Parsley plant

This plant was the new growth off the remainder of a root of a plant that was rashly pulled the year before. On contact it rejected the idea of the root being harvested, and implied that it would not go well for being used if it was harvested, due to previous treatment. The plant agreed that its seeds could be harvested when they were ripe. The plant directed me towards the Parsley plant more suitable. (This plant is the subject in example two.)

### *Example Two*

Formal Contact: Wild Parsley plant (the recommended plant from example one).

Contacted for the purpose of harvesting whole plant and root for medicinal purposes.

Intelligence Appearance: Feminine, young, lithe.

Signs Given: The element grade signs in the following

order—Air, Water, then Air, then the Intelligence repeated the Air sign to confirm the dominant element.

Report from conversation: I was told not to pull out by the hand but to tie something soft around the stalk. Told to clear a particular weed away (dandelion). It agreed to having a Mercury vibration. It agreed to be harvested and to draw as much goodness as possible into its body before harvesting. On the day of harvesting I returned and made contact with the plant 30 minutes prior, asking the plant to prepare itself and release its hold on the ground; the plant seemed apprehensive, so I projected love towards it and promised to plant seed. At the time of harvesting the root came out with ease. Although I was prepared for this it was still a surprise due to difficulties in the past in pulling the same variety.

### Example Three
Formal Contact: Sage Plant in flower.

Intelligence Appearance: About 2'6" high, youth's face and short close-cropped black hair, around ruddy cheeks and purple flowing robe—like a choirboy. This plant was in flower with lavender-purple flowers. Purpose of contact was just to converse.

Signs Given: Water, Air, then Earth—Water again confirming the dominant element.

Conversation: Sage—'We do not have names, we are known by essences—you will know me as the 'Spirit of the Sage in Flower'.'

Adept—'How much life has this Sage?'

Sage—'Life is eternal, we will not die.'

Adept—'Tell me about your growth.'

Sage—'You've planted me in a sour place, we need lime, turn the earth around my roots. You do not harvest me in time before the bud. I am in harmony with those around, plant my seed . . .'

### Example Four
Formal Contact: Alehoof herb.

Plant was amongst other plants (weeds and grasses) and was in flower. Some of the leaves did not look overly healthy—it was late in the season. Purpose of contact was just to converse.

Intelligence Appearance: slim built, feminine male (youth) soft pink mauve colour (same colour as flowers), light brown hair.

Signs Given: Earth as the dominant element, then Fire and Water.

Planets Given: Jupiter's vibrations were favoured by the Intelligence.

Conversation: It said its magical properties were the benefits it gives to other plants that grow near it. It is of help to sheep—their liver and kidneys, and aids the eyes of sheep. Generally good for horses but the animals only eat it if they need it. For humans it is good for blood (the roots and flowers), the leaves for bruises. It is a happy little plant and reaches out for others to be in happiness.

### Example Five
Informal Contact: Rosemary Plant in flower

'I was feeling devitalised and was wondering what to do about it. On looking outside I saw the sun was shining so went into the back yard in the hope the sun would help revitalise my energies. Once outside, soaking up the sun and not feeling any better, I was drawn to a grass spot beside a Rosemary shrub which had been flowering since late Autumn and right through mid-winter, which it was at this time. Before I realised what was happening, I was engaged in a conversation with the plant which had developed a soft haze about it. (Note that prior contact had been made with this particular plant 6 months earlier.) The Rosemary Intelligence was asking me what was wrong and then it told me to put my face up close to it and inhale its scent, gently stroke its branches and get its scent on my hands. Then it encouraged me to eat a couple of its tiny purple/lavender flowers. This was a surprise to me, as at the time I did not know its flowers were edible. I decided such a small quantity would do me no harm so followed all instructions. From the moment the flowers went into my mouth a burning sensation began and an immediate revitalization of energies took over. My exhaustion lifted. I then continued to sit in the sun by the plant sharing a few eternal moments.'

*Caution*: Rosemary flowers, or the Rosemary plant itself, eaten raw especially but used in teas, etc., is poisonous in large doses. One or two tiny flowers are enough.

### Miscellaneous

Reportings of informal contact made by plants to people and people to plants are quite common now, and if you bother to listen hard enough you will hear your own plants talk to you, if you bothered to acknowledge them in the first place. Have you ever felt a drawing feeling, looked over to a plant and realised it needed watering?

### Expanding the Sphere of Sensation to the Vegetable Kingdom

Astral method of contact with herbal life force.

### Stage 1

A    Have in mind the chosen purpose for which you require the herb, along with your decision on the method which you will be using; e.g. drying, powdering, sachet, oil extraction (and method of extraction) etc., along with all astrological and other calculations as to times of commencement. Prior knowledge of all this is vital. If there is no decisive intent of purpose and method, the following may not have the necessary and appropriate response from the herb which is to be contacted.

**B**    Choose the herb:
1. by 'correspondence' (its attributions) to the purpose.
2. perform lesser banishing ritual around oneself. Be cleansed of all other thoughts but one's intent.
3. call down the D.W.B.
4. go out into one's garden where presumably the herb will be growing, or go to the area where one knows such a herb grows.
5. give a prayer to the elementals (all elements)—see below.
(*note*: feel each element as one invokes it, e.g. immerse one's aura in the sensation of the element.)

'I come in the Power of the Light. I come in the Mercy of the Light. I come in the Light of Wisdom. The Light hath healing in its Wings. Yea come thou forth, I mightly conjure thy radiant perfection to compel All Spirits to be subject unto me.

In the name of Michael (Mee-chah-ale), the great archangel of Fire, and in the Kerubic sign of Leo the Lion (*make sign*), Spirits of Fire Adore your Creator! I invite the Great King of Fire, the Immortal, Eternal, Ineffable and Uncreated Father of All, borne upon the Chariots of Worlds, which ever roll in ceaseless motion, Thy Majesty, Golden, Vast and Eternal, Shineth above the Heaven of Stars. Above them thou art exalted, I Invoke Thee, I Adore Thee and every Spirit of the all rushing Fire to give blessings and help me in my purpose. (*give Fire grade sign*)

In the name of Gabriel (Gah-bree-ale) the great archangel of water, and in the sign of the Eagle (*give sign of eagle*), Spirits of Water, Adore your Creator! I invite the Terrible King of the Sea, King of the Deluge and of the Rains of Spring. Thou who commandest moisture which is, as it were, the Blood of the Earth, to become the Sap of the Plants, I Invoke Thee, I Adore Thee, and every Spirit of the Water to give blessings and help me in my purpose. (*give Water grade sign*)

In the name of Raphael (Rah-phah-ale) the great archangel of the air, and in the Kerubic Sign of the Head of

Man (*give sign of Aquarius*), Spirits of Air Adore your Creator! I invite the King of Air, Spirit of Life, Spirit of Wisdom, whose breath giveth forth and withdraweth the form of All Things. Invoke Thee, Adore Thee, and every Spirit of the Ether, and of the Whirling Air to give Blessings and to help me in my purpose. (*give Air grade sign*)

In the name of Auriel (Awe-ree-ale), the great archangel of Earth, and by the sign of the Head of the Ox (*give sign of Taurus*), Spirits of Earth Adore your Adoni! I invite the Invisible King of Earth, who, taking the Earth for Foundation, didst hollow its depths to fill them with Thy Almighty Power. Thou whose name shaketh the arches of the World, rewarder of the subterranean workers, I Invoke Thee, I Adore Thee, and every Spirit upon the Earth and Under the Earth and of the Stable Land, to give blessings and help me in my purpose.' (*give Earth grade sign*)

Give LVX signs

Remain silent and contemplate the presence of the elements.

6. stand a distance from the growing herbs, sending forth your message (or your purpose and intent) by mind reaching— extension of aura—out to the herbs, and of the herb of your choice, calling forth for the herb most in harmony to the vibrations of your message and purpose to send an answer back (reciprocate aura extension and make contact). You should feel very intense vibrations from the source *drawing* you in the direction until you actually stand beside the herb, focusing on it.

There will be occasions when the herb that one had previously chosen is not the one that answers the call. In this event the operation is not stopped at that point; one identifies the herb, if not then, between stage one and two. Its attributions are identified as well, but if they do not correspond, do not despair. This is a case where nature is telling you the true vibrations of that particular plant. The vibrations of other plants of the species may not be of that vibration, therefore do not generalise after your discovery. Many factors are taken into consideration as to why that herb answered your vibration. But, you must be sure that the operation had not gone wrong; therefore, always double check by repeating Stage 1 'A & B' two more times on different days. If the same result arises, then you know it to be true. Then you may proceed to steps 'C' and 'D'. If step 'D' is failed (i.e. answers contrary to the nature of the chosen operation) then one ceases and returns on another more harmonious day, and in more harmonious conditions, starting Stage 1 from the beginning as one did before attempting the herbal search.

**C**      Draw a magical circle around the plant in question, vibrating names of art—by will alone or with the magical sword—then draw a circle around yourself where you chose to stand back from the herb. Purify and consecrate area around plant, and purify area around plant of any element which could harm the operation.

**D**      Evoke the elemental of the herb which answered your call to come forth and show itself, and thereby you will be able to identify by the image and clothing as to whether this elemental is of the nature of your proposed working, also demanding the grade sign of its element on appearance—most important. If grade sign is not given and appearance not in accordance, abandon the exercise, as given further on.

This invocation is done by 'Will' power, silent or spoken, with the use of the element weapon (imaginary or real, depending on whether you are in a private area or not and can afford to let others see what you are doing) of the element nature of one's proposed operation. You can adopt your own words or the following, drawing the zodiac signs (shown in brackets) in the air with your right index finger and thumb:

'I command ye Spirit of this Plant (name) before me by the

names of
Michael (Mee-chahale) the great archangel of Fire (♌)
Gabriel (Gah-bree-ale) the great archangel of Water (♋) (♏),
Raphael (Rah-phah-ale) the great archangel of Air (♒),
and
Auriel (Awe-ree-ale) the great archangel of Earth (♉),
to show yourself and your nature before me now, and to giveth
me the sign of your element as I giveth you my sign.'
'Appear'!! (When the elemental appears give the sign of your
grade in silence.)

To aid the appearance of the elemental use your will and
visualisation. The appearance that normally manifests is not
one that is seen by the naked eye, although this is possible, but
one seen by the inner eye. Normally a dense haze appears in
the drawn circle above the plant, and encompassing the plant.

**E** When identification is made to your satisfaction, you
inform the elemental of your purpose and operation, *when and
how* you will be harvesting the plant (stating most of Stage 2)
and commanding the elemental to prepare the plant for what
is to take place, and to show the Adept where the plant is to be
picked (if picking is to take place), or any other instructions
from the elemental concerning the method of harvesting. The
elemental's instructions *must* be followed to the letter, if the
operation is to continue and succeed, but do be sure that the
elemental is not having fun with you.
**F** Give notice of departure, seal off area, do banishing
ritual of pentagram, thus sealing yourself off. Leave the site of
the herb and prepare for Stage 2, which can be done on the
same day, but no sooner than 30 minutes from departure, and
preferably on another day of suitable harmonies astrologically
or otherwise.

### Stage 2

**A**     Before or on day of harvesting, clear ground around the herb of surrounding weeds.

**B**     30 minutes to an hour before harvesting do lesser banishing pentagram ritual, then make astral contact with herb, informing it that you are actually going ahead with the operation and at what time.

**C**     At time of harvesting draw another circle around area, vibrating names of art.

**D**     Place yourself downwind of the herb (if possible) and feel the biological changes and adjustments the herb made and makes—if it needs help, assist it with your aura to isolate the energies you require from it.

**E**     By now you should know exactly where it is to be picked—or whatever the operation—but first test the area to be sure of the place, by placing the fingers and thumb of your left hand near the area (but not touching the plant). You should sensitize (feel) a cold spot.

**F**     Harvest according to the rules as previously explained.

# BIBLIOGRAPHY

Albertus, Frater. *Alchemists' Handbook*, Samuel Weiser Inc.

Barbaut, Armand. *Gold of a Thousand Mornings*, Neville Spearman, London.

Beedell, Suzanne. *Herbs for Health & Beauty*, Sphere Books Ltd.

Bills, Rex E. *The Rulership Book*, Macoy Publishing & Masonic Supply Company Inc.

Carter, Charles E.O. *The Principles of Astrology*, 'Quest' Theosophical Publishing House.

Clynes, S., B.Sc. & Williams, D.J.W., M.A. *General School Chemistry*, The English Universities Press Ltd.

Cyran, Henry B. *The Australian/N.Z. Book of Herbs*, C&H.

Daath, Heinrich. *Medical Astrology*, Lyncroft Gardens.

Dee, John, Dr. *The Hieroglyphic Monad*, Samuel Weiser Inc.

Eagle, Robert. *Herbs, Useful Plants*, BBC Publications.

*Encyclopedia of Science and Technology*, McGraw-Hill.

Jacobs, Betty E.M. *Growing and Using Herbs Successfully*, Garden Way Publishing.

Lapidus. *In Pursuit of Gold, Alchemy today in theory and practice*, Samuel Weiser Inc.

Lust, John, N.D., D.B.M. *The Herb Book*, Bantam Books.

Mathers, MacGregor. *Key of Solomon*, Samuel Weiser Inc.

*Potential Crops for Processing in NZ III, Part III* (of V parts) 'Herbs, Spices & Essential Oil'. Information Series IPD.IS/ 10, Department of Scientific & Industrial Research NZ, June 1979.

Robson, Vivian E., B.Sc. *The Fixed Stars and Constellations in Astrology*, Samuel Weiser Inc.

*The Rodale Herb Book*, Rodale Press.

Rose, Jeanne. *Herbs and Things*, Grosset & Dunlap Worman Publishing Coy New York.

Shah, Indries. *The Secret Lore of Magic*, Abacus, Sphere Books Ltd.

Smith, Keith Vincent. *The Illustrated Earth Garden Herbal, a herbal companion*, Thomas Nelson Australia Pty Ltd.

Starhawk. *The Spiral Dance*, Harper & Row Publishers.

Thomson, William A.R., M.D. (Editor). *Healing Plants—A Modern Herbal*.

Unpublished manuscripts of the Golden Dawn from 'Whare Ra' and 'Thoth/Hermes' temples, New Zealand.

Vogh, James. *The Cosmic Factor*, Granada-Hart, Davis, Mac-Gibbon.

Warburton, Diana. *Magiculture, a book of Garden Charms*, Prism Press.